MW00942049

Earliest Teachable Moment

Personal Safety for Babies, Toddlers, and Preschoolers

Irene van der Zande

Copyright Information

Earliest Teachable Moment: Personal Safety for Babies, Toddlers, and Preschoolers. Copyright © Irene van der Zande October 2013. All rights reserved. No part of this publication may be reproduced in any form or by any electronic or mechanical means, including information storage and retrieval systems, without prior signed written permission from the Author or her designated representative. First edition.

Use of Materials

With proper acknowledgement, readers are encouraged to use knowledge from the Kidpower program about self-protection, confidence building, advocacy, personal safety, and self-defense strategies and skills in their personal lives and professional activities. We ask that readers tell people about Kidpower Teenpower Fullpower International when they use any examples, ideas, stories, language, and practices that they learned from our program, and let others know how to reach our organization.

Restrictions

Unless people or agencies have an active certification and ongoing relationship with Kidpower Teenpower Fullpower International, they are not authorized to represent themselves or give the appearance of representing themselves as working under our organization's auspices.

This means that individuals and groups must have an active certification or agreement with our organization to be authorized to teach, promote or organize workshops or other presentations using the Kidpower, Teenpower, Fullpower program names, workshop names, reputation or credentials. Please visit the Kidpower Teenpower Fullpower International web site or call our office for information about our instructor certification and center development programs.

Liability Disclaimer

Each situation is unique, and we can make no guarantee about the safety or effectiveness of the content or techniques described in this material. We do not accept liability for any negative consequences from use of this material.

Earliest Teachable Moment

Table of Contents

Table of Contents

Introduction

From the moment babies are born, we are protecting them from harm and teaching them what it means to be safe with their feelings and their bodies. We hold their heads out of the water in the bath. We reassure them when they become upset or scared. We strap them into car seats even if they don't like it.

As young children start to move around and become able to understand, we start to teach them how to be safe themselves. We tell a young toddler, "Hot" and to stay away from the heater. We hold a three-year-old's hands firmly when we cross the street. We remind kids to wash their hands before eating.

In the same way, we are constantly teaching children how to be safe with people. Fire safety means much more than just burning prevention – it also means knowing how to enjoy fire for warmth and cooking. Personal safety means much more than being safe from bullying, violence, and abuse – it also means developing strong relationships with people so we can enjoy each other.

This book is designed for busy parents and caregivers of young children who might want to read it all the way through or look in the table of contents and go right to a particular chapter or article. Each section is set up to stand on its own without depending on prior chapters.

When it comes to safety, the earliest teachable moment is the best teachable moment, as long as this is done in a way that builds understanding, skills, and habits without creating anxiety or fear. This book uses principles and practices from Kidpower's almost 25 years of teaching positive and effective personal safety skills to people of all ages and abilities to provide an introductory handbook for parents and caregivers of babies, toddlers, and pre-schoolers.

Here are Kidpower's 7 keys to teaching safety skills to everyone, everywhere:

- **Stay calm.** Because anxiety does not make anyone safer; it just makes people worried and distracts them from learning.

- **Make it fun.** Because enthusiastic, vivid, upbeat teachers make learning joyful instead of difficult.

- **Make it simple.** Because simple things are easier to remember.

- **Be consistent.** Because consistent messages make more sense.

- **Practice – a lot!** Because repeated, successful practice makes skills stronger and increases confidence.

- **Make it relevant.** Because people learn a skill faster when it seems useful.

- **Stay in charge.** Because leaders are responsible for the safety of those in their care or under their supervision as well as for ensuring that their actions are safe and respectful to others. Powerful, respectful adult leadership is essential in guiding children to use safety skills in their daily lives and in protecting them from harm.

I hope that this book will provide parents and caregivers of small children with useful guidance about how to use these keys to have more fun, greater safety, and fewer problems with people in their families, day care centers, and early childhood programs.

Emotional Safety
For New Parents

Earliest Teachable Moment

There is a joke that you should enjoy the confidence you have as a parent just before your first child is born, because this is the last time you will feel that confident until you are a grandparent!

That was certainly true for me. When I was pregnant with my first child, I knew where she was and who was with her. Even though I couldn't see her, I felt strongly that all was well with her.

And then, all of a sudden, I was holding this tiny precious new being in my arms, utterly vulnerable and totally dependent on me. Like many new parents, I was breathless with joy, punctuated by brief bouts of terror.

My husband Ed was almost as scared as I was, but he figured that I probably knew what I was doing. After I called our doctor five times in the first three days of our baby's life, he persuaded me to join a support group for new mothers.

When their adults feel safe, children are also more likely to feel safe. Belief is one of the most powerful personal safety tools we have. Protecting ourselves from experiences that undermine positive beliefs is important for our own safety and well-being.

For example, when I was pregnant with our second child, Ed became very worried about the teacher of the review childbirth class we had started. After the first night, he said, "We're not going back. That teacher keeps telling stories about women who have had to have cesareans. You're so suggestible that I am afraid you'll worry yourself into making this happen."

We found a different class that met our specific needs rather than dwelling on all the possible problems. This teacher discussed self-care during pregnancy for parents who already have a young child and talked about how to prepare an older sibling for the arrival of a new baby. We learned the important lesson that pregnant women have the right to set boundaries about what others say to them as well as about what is done to their bodies.

Sometimes people treat pregnant women as if their bodies belong to the human species as a whole rather than to the women themselves. This is why we offer a special practice for pregnant women in our boundary workshops.

For example, suppose that Cornelia is our instructor, and Lois is our pregnant student. Cornelia pretends to be a family friend. She comes up to Lois and starts gushing, "Hi! How exciting! When is your baby due?" As Cornelia talks, she starts to pat Lois's belly.

With some coaching, Lois removes Cornelia's hands and holds them away from her, as she answers cheerfully, "In about three months."

"Oh, you poor thing!" Cornelia keeps gushing, thoughtlessly. "I can tell by how you're carrying the baby that you will have a hard birth. I remember when…."

Lois doesn't want to hear any horror stories about birth, so she interrupts and says firmly, "I don't want to talk about that. My doctor says that everything is fine."

Cornelia says, "Yes, of course, all you want is a healthy baby. Unfortunately, with all the pollution now, you never know what terrible things might happen to the baby."

Lois doesn't want to hear any horror stories about that either, so she interrupts again and says, "I don't want to hear about bad things happening to babies. I believe that my baby is healthy and fine."

Lois then changes the subject by asking Cornelia to talk about herself, which is something Cornelia is happy to do.

These boundary-setting skills are also useful after a baby is born. For example, parents might want to practice stopping well-meaning people from making negative comments about how their child is developing. Or, they might want to practice stopping friendly people in public who keep commenting or even try to touch their baby. And, stopping other family members from forcing attention and affection on a young child is a common issue.

You should be in charge of choosing who touches your child. Before they can speak well, and often even after they can, you will need to help speak for them to set boundaries.

Parents have very different feelings when it comes to their comfort about who holds their babies, who is allowed to hug and kiss them and games surrounding touch such as tickling or rough-housing. Take the time to discuss with your partner and other caregivers of your child what you want your family rules to be.

One family decided that they did not want anyone they didn't know touching their young children. Upholding this standard often took some calm, friendly, but also assertive maneuverers when out in public. For example, when shopping in a large store, the father holding his one year old encountered a nice older man who started wanting to tickle his son's toes.

"I'm going to get those cute toes!" said the man.

"Oh, no you aren't!" responded the dad in a very cheerful tone while moving away very quickly.

Knowledge is power, but opinions are confusing

People used to believe that having a baby automatically meant that you knew how to raise a child and that becoming a grandparent automatically meant that you were the world's leading expert. Of course, that theory is rarely true, but in some ways, it made life simpler.

As a species, our ideas about what is important for the well-being of our young have evolved. Ideas about what is best for a baby keep changing, and many things that our own parents believed are now in question. New parents are bombarded with often-conflicting information. Every aspect of parenting has expert advice available.

- "Let her cry."

- "Pick her up."

- "Go lie down with her."

- "Put her in your bed."

- "Don't put her in your bed."

Most of the time, new parents are confused – and too often, they are overwhelmed and anxious. Children are best off when their new parents feel empowered to take care of both their babies and themselves.

Steps to confidence for new parents

Gather information. Many wonderful books cover all the aspects of parenting, and the Internet has a wealth of resources. Learn as much as you can. Remember that expert health and child-rearing advice often keeps changing. Find information that reflects your own values rather than believing something just because it is highly recommended or currently popular.

Earliest Teachable Moment

Useful resources available on line and in libraries include pediatrician Dr. Harvey Karp's *Happiest Baby on the Block* and *Happiest Toddler on the Block* website, books, and DVDs with his very practical suggestions for how to nurture children and to calm an upset child. Also, my first book, *1,2,3, The Toddler Years*, is used by parents and caregivers worldwide – and child development pioneer Magda Gerber's *Resources for Infant Educarers* website provides books and training showing how to use her respect for infants philosophy in daily life.

Listen to yourself. No one knows your baby or you as well as you do. Every individual is unique, and the right answer for one person is not the right answer for everyone. Try to separate your intuition from your triggers so that you are making decisions based on what you truly feel rather than on anxiety.

Accept Differences. Worrying because our kids are different than other children is a major pitfall to confidence as a parent. Comparing our kids to those of our relatives and friends or just other kids we see with parents at the park is normal but can undermine our emotional safety. Children come into this world with their own personalities, needs, sensitivities, levels of energy, and ways of learning. They often develop at different rates. To stay emotionally safe, try to recognize that judgmental thoughts like "Why isn't my child like that child?" or "What did I or am I doing wrong to make my child be this way?" are not useful.

Get support. True support comes from people who treat you with respect. Support means listening to you, making suggestions in a non-pushy way, and offering help when you want it. Unless the safety of your child is actually at stake, support does not mean repeating unwanted advice, overriding your choices, making constant worried comments, or insisting that certain ways of doing things are the only right way to do them.

If your parents or other adult family members are supportive people, have them involved in your child's life as much as possible. If not, have them involved in ways that work for your baby and for you.

Find other parents to talk with who also have young children. Baby and toddler groups can be wonderful ways to meet people who share your child-rearing philosophy, help you and your child build friendships, and let you spend time with other people who are probably very interested in talking about all the ins and outs of babies and parenting.

Helping Young Children Understand Personal Boundaries And Develop Positive Relationships

As babies, toddlers, and preschoolers become more independent and move on their own out in the world, parents often ask questions like," How do I teach my child about personal boundaries? How do I help my child to develop positive relationships with others, both adults and kids?"

Children have different temperaments, and their behavior is likely to change at different stages of development. What works best is to make decisions based on your understanding of your own child and to be willing to change your plan, without comparing this child to other kids or to what he or she was like before. Is this child a social butterfly or very reserved and slow to warm up to others? Does this child need lots of downtime or lots of action? Does this child try extremely hard to follow the rules or does this child seem to need to define boundaries by pushing against them?

Children are constantly learning about relationships and boundaries from their adults, so we must set a good example by having positive relationships and healthy boundaries ourselves. Even if a baby doesn't understand, he or she will respond to stress, tone of voice, and body language.

To have positive relationships, you need to have healthy boundaries, which means:

- Recognizing what is and is not safe and respectful both emotionally and physically.

- Knowing your rights and being able to speak up about what is and is not okay with you.

- Knowing how to be careful with your body and your words, so that you don't cross the boundaries of others.

- Knowing that all of your feelings are okay, but that you

can learn how to express your feelings in ways that are not destructive to others.

- Knowing how to advocate for the rights of others to help make the world a safer, happier place for everyone.

As soon as they can move around and begin to under-stand, children can be coached in learning about different kinds of social boundaries. Start with noticing and appreciating what each child CAN do and then build from there. Even if you have to guide the child every single time for a few years, these lessons are being absorbed.

A crawling baby who wants to pet a cat needs close supervision as she is coached verbally and physically to "be gentle" - and children can learn to "be gentle" when touching anyone. Even at young ages, children need to start to learn about NOT touching sometimes. You don't touch the stove because it's "HOT!" You can jump on Daddy, but not when he's ill. Many things are okay to touch, but NOT put in your mouth.

As they develop more speech and understanding, toddlers can start to use very simple skills to protect their own boundaries and respect the boundaries of others. For example:

- "Say, 'Please stop. I don't like that.'"

- "Listen to his words."

- "Give her more room."

- "Move away."

- "Throw those hurting words away."

- "Use your Mouth Closed Power."

- "Use your Hands Down Power."

- "Say, 'I'm using that now. You can have it when I'm done.'"

- "It's my turn now. You'll have to wait your turn."

Being polite by acknowledging people socially is an adult need, not a child's. We believe that younger children should not have to engage socially with adults until they feel ready. Children can learn to greet an adult when you say it's okay by making eye contact, waving, shaking hands, and saying, "Hello" or "Good-bye." However, this should be suggested gently rather than forced.

If a child finds greeting new people to be difficult, the best plan is to model the behavior yourself and to let the child decide to greet others in his or her own way at his or her own pace. If an adult is a family member or close friend, you might need to explain to this person that the rule in your family is that children don't have to hug or kiss anyone or sit on anyone's lap unless they want to.

The mother of three-year-old Rosa found that upholding a child's right to refuse affection can be hard to do. "I had to tell my aunt to stop asking Rosa to give her a kiss. To her it was kind of a game, but she really didn't like it. My aunt's feelings were hurt for a long time, even though I explained that I didn't want Rosa ever to feel that she had to give affection just because an adult said so."As adults, we need to know that most of the people who harm children are people they know. The good news is that good supervision and strong boundaries can prevent most abuse.

The Kidpower Boundary Rules are:

- **We each belong to ourselves.** Show children that their bodies are important and deserve to be treated with love and respect. Help them to stop unwanted tickling, roughhousing, teasing, or affection. As children get older, start to teach them the safety rules about private areas, but toddlers are too young for this to make sense to them.

- **Some things are not a choice.** Especially things for health and safety are not a choice. Whether they like it or not, we need to hold a child's hand when crossing the street until the child can cross safely on her or his own.

- **Problems should not be secrets.** Touch should not be a secret. Games should not be a secret. Presents should not be a secret. Secrecy is a major reason that child abuse can continue. Teach young children not to keep secrets.

- **Keep telling until you get help.** Letting children know that they can count on us for help can make a huge difference. When they try to tell us something, we can stop what we're doing and pay attention. By having that kind of relationship with us now, they'll be far more likely to come to us later if someone tries to harm them.

The reality is that adults are often busy and distracted - and children do need to learn to wait if they want something. However, even young children can be encouraged to be polite and persistent in interrupting a busy adult if they have a safety problem.

Children get a very mixed message about their personal boundaries when they are pressured to act affectionately towards someone against their will. Our Kidpower rule is that touch, teasing, or play for fun or affection should be:

- **Safe**

- **The choice of each person**

- **Allowed by the grown-ups in charge**

- **Never a secret**

As described below, we can teach young children how to use these boundary rules in daily life by using toys or puppets to act out different safety problems and solutions. We can have them practice using each of these rules in simple games. Make these practices fun rather than scary. For example, the safety problem can be another child or puppet gently pulling the child's hair rather than an adult doing something upsetting.

How To Choose Safe People To Care For Your Children

Children can benefit in many ways when they are cared for by different people:

- Often child care helps secure a better income for the family.

- Kids can learn how to be close to people who are not their parents.

- They can have the chance to learn and play with other children in a child-oriented environment.

At the same time, having harm come to their children is the nightmare of all the adults who love them. Worried parents ask questions like, "How can I make sure that the people I trust to care for my children will keep them safe and well?"

Danger can come in many forms, including in the form of poor judgment. A heart-breaking tragedy happened in San Jose, a city near my home. A baby-sitter entrusted with the care of a toddler left him with her roommate for a short time. The roommate walked over the train tracks with the toddler and then told the toddler to wait while she went back to get her baby in the stroller. Instead, the child followed her back across the tracks and was killed by a train.

Children are extremely vulnerable to injury or abuse as a result of the choices of the people who are taking care of them. Even with caregivers from accredited programs, abusive behavior is a risk. While a nanny was caring for a family's baby, her boyfriend visited her. The baby's family did not know that he was going to be there. The boyfriend got drunk and lost his temper, throwing the little boy against a wall.

Children are not born knowing how to take care of themselves. If they are not adequately supervised by responsible people making safe choices, children sometimes bully others or get bullied, molest others or get molested, wander off, climb up too high and fall, drown in even a couple of inches of water, get hit by cars, eat poisonous substances, and play with fire.

We don't expect children to learn to play a sport well without hours of practice and adults helping them to learn. The same is true for safety skills.

Children need adults to protect them until they have the skills, understanding, and capability to protect themselves. This means having adults close by and paying attention, especially in public places. A few years ago, a grandmother sat inside the house while her young granddaughters, ages five and three, played outside by the street. Suddenly, a man drove up, jumped out of his car, and kidnapped the older girl before the grandmother realized what was happening.

The good news is that dangers from caregivers can almost always be prevented. Letting someone else take care of the children we love means trusting this person with the most precious part of our lives. Parents and guardians are responsible for selecting and supervising the care of their children, whether the caregivers are individuals or the staff of programs such as child care centers and schools.

At the same time, it is important to keep your balance. You do not want to overreact to an upsetting possibility in a way that damages your child's trust in being left with other people.

For example, there was a three-year-old girl who loved to give herself and other children hickeys by sucking on the skin all over their arms and legs. The teacher worked hard to stop this behavior, but the children enjoyed the interesting phenomena of seeing red-brown spots emerge on their bodies. The teacher addressed the issue in circle time, with all the children's parents, and with the little girl directly.

Parents reacted very differently to this problem. Some were respectful and helped the teacher work on solutions. Others were angry and demanded that the little girl be forced to leave, which would have prevented her from learning how to change her behavior. One parent got so upset that she removed her own child from the program, depriving him of a loving, educational place with a teacher he adored. Eventually, the combined efforts succeeded in stopping the hickeys. What was important was that the problem was addressed effectively without being ignored and without panic.

It is the job of adults to ensure that the environments where we put children and the people we entrust with their care are emotionally and physically safe. We recommend that adults have high expectations in assessing other caregivers in terms of the following standards.

- Good cleanliness practices – especially with food preparation, handling of illness, and toilet/bathroom practices – to prevent disease from spreading.

- Age-appropriate protection from hazards such as traffic, poisonous substances, sharp objects, water, fire, potentially dangerous people, and getting lost.

- Clear boundaries about touch, teasing, and play between all adults and children. This means that anything for fun or affection must be the choice of each person involved, safe, and allowed by the adults in charge. This also means that any touch required (such as touch for health or cleanliness) is known to the parents or guardians and is never a secret.

- Effective, respectful behavior management so that children are guided into interacting with others in positive ways and stopped when they are using destructive behavior without being punished, called names, or yelled at. This must include a clear action plan for dealing with violent, hurtful, or unsafe behavior that is shared with all staff, parents, and, to the level they can understand, with the children. The goal is to have a step-by-step process for addressing unsafe or hurtful behavior that is effective in stopping this behavior without being shaming.

- Adequate supervision so that adults see what is happening with children, make sure that children are where they are supposed to be, and step in to help children solve problems positively rather than destructively.

- Specific permission from parents and guardians about any changes in terms of who will be with their children, what they will be doing, and where they will be going.

- Age-appropriate activities that will help the child to learn and to grow.

- Permission for older children to always be able to call you if they need help.

- At schools, camps, or youth groups, clear policies and practices in place about preventing bullying, molestation, and other violence. Make sure that they do background checks to verify that their staff members have no history of being convicted of abuse or other dangerous behavior. However, remember that background checks are not enough since most child molesters and others dangerous to kids have not yet been caught.

People and organizations are not perfect, and situations sometimes change. Supervise the care of your children by taking these actions:

- **Research carefully who will be with your children.** Ask for ideas and recommendations from others. Look around. Is the home or room for younger children childproof? Is the atmosphere child-friendly? Are your concerns respectfully and comprehensively addressed? Or, do you feel talked down to as though you are worrying unnecessarily? If you do not know someone well, consider getting a background check

- **Take the time to keep checking in, including making unexpected visits.** You should always have easy access to your children and be welcomed into their environments. If your child plays happily and then gets upset by seeing you, you can still monitor what is going on by staying out of sight.

- **Raise concerns right away about any potential problems.** Give feedback promptly, firmly, and respectfully. Insist on getting the answers you need. Don't let the fact that a caregiver or teacher has a lot of education, acts in a charming way, or says what you want to hear stop you.

- **Notice changes in personnel, location, policies, and activities that might affect your child.**

- **Be clear about your expectations.** Make sure you know who will be with your child, what your child will be doing, and where your child will be going –and that this person or place will inform you before making changes.

- **Be realistic.** Teachers and child care workers have a very hard job and are often blamed for the behavior of children who come into the group care setting with many problems with boundaries and behavior. While it is the teacher's job to keep control, she or he cannot prevent all hits, hurts, or upset feelings. Look for teachers who are working hard to help children to behave safely and appropriately. Look for teachers who address situations with you directly and who are making progress.

- **Be honest about your own child's behavior.** Even happy healthy children sometimes have bad days or troubles with adjusting to being in a larger group environment. Be willing to hear critical comments about your children's behavior, as these comments are designed to help your child be as successful as possible. Critical comments about specific behavior with a plan or question on how to help are appropriate. Critical comments that attack a child's character or make unrealistic demands on you are not appropriate.

- **Make sure that you really understand what is going on.** If you think there is a problem, don't jump to conclusions and get upset. Give yourself enough time to assess what is happening and what needs to be done. Go and observe for yourself.

- **Treat issues that relate to the emotional and physical safety for your child as urgent.** Don't let fear of causing hurt feelings, embarrassment, offense, or inconvenience to anyone stop you from speaking up for your child's safety and self-esteem.

- **Express appreciation for what goes well.** Teachers and child care staff are usually underpaid and overworked. Most of them are very loving and committed to the well-being of the children in their care. Make sure you let them know how much you appreciate what they do for your child and your family.

Too often, people dismiss legitimate concerns by using a negative label such as "overprotective" or "paranoid." If someone says this to you, you can say proudly, "Thank you! I am just doing my job!" – and then keep insisting on getting the answers you need.

Our responsibility as parents or guardians is to be protective and vigilant, and also allow children the experiences they need to grow into confident,well-rounded, independent young adults. We do not want to let unnecessary anxiety to prevent our kids from having opportunities to be with new people, learn how to get along with others, and go to new places. For guidance in how to figure how what is truly protective and what is not in our child's best interest, see *Helicopters or Protectors? - How to keep your kids safe without unhelpful hovering* in the Appendix.

Checking First To Be Safe With Objects, Animals, Strangers, And Other Potential Problems

Young children do not have the understanding, skills, or life experience to be left on their own without adult protection. This means that, when we are caring for a young child, we must split our attention even if we are trying to get something else done – such as shopping, texting, or talking with someone - so that we know where they are, who is with them, and what they are doing.

Young children are safest when they know to Move Away and Check First with you or another caregiver anytime they encounter something or someone that is unfamiliar to them – be it a shiny piece of broken glass, an interesting book of matches, a very red pill, a cute bug, a furry animal, or a friendly person.

Rewarding children for pointing rather than touching or eating something unfamiliar helps this behavior to become a habit. Since young children sometimes pick up things that adults don't see, teaching them to give it to the adult right away can also prevent a lot of problems.

One family taught their nine-month-old to give them any little toys, coins or other things she founded in the carpet and was rewarded for doing so with a big clap and cheer. She then eagerly gave her parents potentially unsafe objects rather than trying to eat them. Children can also learn to Check First before running off on their own or before hiding.

Even though children are most likely to be harmed by people they know and by preventable accidents, many parents are most worried about what to teach their children about strangers.

It is very unfortunate that in English the word "stranger" rhymes with "danger" because the "Stranger Danger" concept promotes fear without making children safer. Instead, once they can understand, we want to teach children about Stranger Safety and Stranger Awareness.

When your children are together with you, you can tell them when it's okay with you for them to say "Hello" or wave to a stranger, to take something from a stranger or, if they wish, even to shake someone's hand. The rule is that YOU get to decide when it's okay and when it's not. Kids might protest, but they are used to the idea that grown-ups get to decide lots of things that they can't.

The reality is that the Stranger Safety Rules are different when children are with their adults or when they are on their own – and this difference can be confusing. When your children are with you, they can do all sorts of things with all sorts of people as long as this is okay with you.

However, small children are only truly with you when they are touching you or within your immediate reach, and you are paying attention. If you are even a little ways away from them and get distracted for even a moment, they are on their own. Consider how far away you would leave a bag with a lot of money in it, and how much attention you would pay. Your young child has little more ability to stay safe than the bag, and is far more valuable.

Young children are safest, especially in public, when they are together with their parents or other adult caregivers. Teach your children to "Stay Together" and remind them before you go out in public, starting from when you get out of the car or bus.

In our Starting Strong workshops, we practice by telling everyone to imagine being at the store or some other public place where the adults are busy shopping. We coach adults to move quickly around the room, pre-tending to look at one thing and then change directions to look at something else or stop to say, "Hi" to someone. We coach the kids to stick to their grown-up "like glue" as they run around the room.

With younger children, you can start teaching them about Stranger Safety by introducing the safety rules with animals they don't know well and then applying these same rules for people they don't know well. The safety rule is that children need to check with their grown-ups first before they get close to an animal or play with an animal, unless they know that animal very, very well.

Once children are old enough to understand, you can practice Checking First using stuffed animals. Play the Check First game by letting the child know where they are – the park of the playground and where their grown-up is – perhaps on the park bench. Pretend to have the animal approach the child and coach the child to move away and check first. Their adult can say, "Thank you for checking first. Let's ask the owner." Or, "Thank you for checking first. A squirrel is a wild animal so let's just watch."

You can then teach children that the Safety Rules with strangers are the same as with animals they don't know well. Because so many young children have already heard about Stranger Danger or gotten other frightening messages, you might need to provide reassurance.

We tell our young students, "A stranger is simply some-one you don't know well. At Kidpower, we believe that most people are GOOD. This means that most strangers are good. You are a stranger to lots of people because they don't know you well, and they are strangers to you because you don't know them well. You don't need to worry. You just need to follow your Safety Plan."

You can teach children that, "When you are on your own, your job is to move away and Check First with your adult before you talk to, take anything from, or get close to a stranger."

You can practice with children by pretending to be a stranger who knows their name, wants to shake hands, let them play with a puppy, or give them a ball. Coach children to move away and tell their grown-up what happened. For example, "A stranger knows my name." The person pretending to be their grown-up can say, "Thank you for checking first. Let's go together."

In settings where children will be encountering lots of people they don't know, tell them what the rules are for that particular setting. For example, "We are going to a neighborhood party where I know lots of people but you might not remember them. You can be close to and say 'Hello' to people anywhere in this room, but don't leave the room without Checking First with me."

Or, "This is the first day of Kindergarten and you are going to meet lots of people for the first time. They are strangers to you and you are strangers to them. The teacher is also a stranger to you right now, and it is okay for you to be with her because I say so. The teacher is the grown-up in charge of keeping you safe when I'm not there, so you can talk with her if you have any problems."

Or, "We are at the park. I am going to sit on this bench and talk with my friend while you play. You can play with kids you don't know, but stay right here in this area and come to me and Check First before you change the plan, Because I am talking and might not hear you, be sure you are holding my hand and looking into my eyes when you Check First."

We also want children to Check First with their adults before they go with anyone, even someone they know. Our goal is that they develop the Check First habit so that they ask you before they change their plan about where they go, who is with them, and what they are doing.

Common Questions About "People Safety" From Parents With Small Children

At Kidpower, we use the term "People Safety" to mean people being safe with and around people. "Fire safety" means much more than just burning prevention – it means being able to use fire safely for warmth, cooking, and enjoyment. And "People Safety" means more than avoiding bullying, violence, and abuse – it means being able to play, learn, and have fun with people.

Some parents worry because their children are "too shy" and will get anxious and withdrawn around people they don't know well. Other parents worry because their children have no discretion and will treat everyone as their new best friend. Some parents worry that their children will be so eager to please that they might be dominated by others. Other parents worry that their children will push against the boundaries of both peers and adults.

Here are some Kidpower answers for some of the concerns that we hear from parents and other caring adults with small children in their lives.

What should I be most worried about in terms of someone who might hurt my child?

At Kidpower, we believe that most people are good. Unfortunately, a few people do very destructive things, which can have a huge impact on everyone's safety.

The reality is that anyone can be a potential danger to a child. Statistically, children are far more likely to be harmed by someone they know than by a stranger, which is why teaching about boundaries is so important.

However, in even the safest of places, there is always a risk that children might be traumatized by getting lost or by having an adult do something dangerous, which is why children need Safety Plans to follow.

On a day-to-day level, children are most likely to deal with social problems such as getting their feelings hurt because they are being left out or someone says something unkind; reacting either too passively or too aggressively when they get frustrated; getting caught up in doing something potentially dangerous together; and not knowing how to persist in getting help from busy adults.

How can I best protect my children's safety before having them be on their own with others for the first time at school or with another group?

There is no substitute for supervising the people who are caring for your children. No matter where your children are, it is important to make sure that the people responsible for their well-being are ensuring a safe, respectful, caring environment where the adults are paying close attention and fully in charge. As they become more verbal, you can also help your children start to learn how to protect their own well-being by giving them a strong foundation of the "People Safety" skills that Kidpower teaches.

Most problems can be prevented if children and their adults have practiced how to ask for help; set boundaries; protect their feelings; stay in charge of their bodies; know their Safety Plan if they get lost; and check first with their grown-ups before they change their plan about where they are going, what they are doing, and who they are with. It's not enough just to tell children what to do; they also need to practice.

How can I encourage my children when they are with groups of children their age at school or elsewhere to get along well with their peers and respect the adults in charge while still taking care of themselves?

Earliest Teachable Moment

Positive boundary-setting skills prepare children (and people of any age) to speak up for themselves and others in respectful, powerful ways. Getting along well means knowing how to ask for what you want and explain what you don't want while understanding that some things are not a choice (e.g. you have to be quiet at circle time or story hour and keep your hands to yourself).

Getting along well also means understanding that you won't always get your way, so you have to listen and learn about other points of view in order to play in ways that are caring and fun for everyone. No matter what, your children need to know that problems should not be secrets and, if they have a problem, their job is to keep asking until they get help.

Having clear rules and understanding how they work help to prevent vulnerability. For example, as children, you learn to wait for the light or crossing guard at the cross walk; you know what the rules are about playing games with friends or at school recess; you know how to throw away hurting words and how to stop yourself from saying hurtful things to others; you know to move away from someone who is not acting safe; you know that touch and games have to be okay with everyone, safe, and allowed; you know how to set boundaries; you know to check first; and you know how to get help when you need it.

What should we be teaching our children about socializing with friends and family?

Some children are very friendly right away, and others are very slow to warm up. We believe that younger children should not have to engage socially with adults or children until they feel ready. Being polite by acknowledging people socially is an adult need, not a child's.

Children can learn to greet an adult they know by making eye contact, waving, shaking hands, and saying, "Hello" or "Good-bye." However, this should be suggested gently rather than forced. If a child finds greeting new people to be difficult, the best plan is to model the behavior yourself and to let the child decide to greet others in his or her own way at his or her own pace.

If an adult is a family member or close friend, you might need to explain to this person that the rule in your family is that children don't have to hug or kiss anyone or sit on anyone's lap unless they want to. Children get a very mixed message about their personal boundaries when they are pressured to be affectionate. Our Kidpower principle is that touch or games for play, teasing, and affection should be the choice of each person, safe, and allowed by the grown-ups in change.

Finally, children are very literal and parents need to be explicit with their children in different settings about what the plan is about where they are going, who is with them, and what they are doing. Except in emergencies where they cannot check first, a child's job is to check first with their parents before changing the plan, even if they are with adults they know.

How can I teach my children about handling emotionally-charged social situations such as being bullied, dealing with name-calling, or other conflicts?

Tell your children that they have the right to be and feel safe everywhere they go – and a responsibility to act safely towards others. If another kid is saying or doing something that is hurtful or scary, their Safety Plan is to speak up if they can – and, if this doesn't work, to leave and to get help.

Children can learn to protect their feelings by throwing hurting words into an imaginary Trash Can and saying something good to themselves.

To use the Kidpower Trash Can Technique, put a hand on one of your hips. Imagine that the hole this makes is your personal trash can. Now, use your other hand to grab in the air as if you are actually catching hurtful words and then throw these words into your personal trash can. Finally, say something nice to yourself aloud as you press your hands against your heart to take in these kind words. This technique is probably our most famous and is so useful that we teach it to adults as well as children.

How can I build my children's social confidence?

Teach your children that life is an adventure and they are heroes who can take charge of their emotional and physical well-being most of the time. The best ways to build confidence of all kinds is to give children opportunities to practice how to handle different kinds of challenges – and to coach them in being successful each step of the way.

Kidpower's Positive Practice teaching method shows how to take situations that are relevant to children, create role-plays that address concerns, adapt for a given child's abilities, and break skills down into achievable steps. For younger children, demonstrations on what to do and not to do can also be very effective when done with toys or puppets.

How can I help my children learn to protect themselves from physical conflicts?

Most physical conflicts can be prevented by proper adult supervision combined with good Kidpower skills for everyone. More aggressive children can learn to be in charge of their bodies and words. More passive children can learn to set clear boundaries and to move away when someone is acting like trouble. For children six and older, we do teach physical self-defense skills to be used ONLY when they are about to be hurt and they cannot leave and get help.

My friends and family members say that I should not get involved when our children have problems, because they believe that kids should be left to just work it out on their own. What do you think?

Until they have the skills to manage problems on their own, children need adult supervision. Most adults will not let children work things out for themselves with cars, fires, knives, or lakes because someone might get hurt. Most adults will not stand by if a child starts throwing blocks through the window or smashing food into the carpet, because this behavior is destructive even if no one is about to get hurt. So why would adults abandon children by expecting them to work things out for themselves when dealing with problems with people?

As adults, we are responsible for creating cultures of caring, respect, and safety for the young people in our lives. Parents of younger children should step in when things start to become unsafe and children are not able to work things out well for themselves. Positive simple interventions can be very effective in teaching children how to speak up for themselves and to listen to others.

For older children, adults can model powerful positive leadership by stepping in to discuss what is going on, stating the values, asking questions to explore whether these values are being met, and exploring options so that everyone can have a good time. At any age, we believe that the most effective consequence of unsafe behavior is for everyone to practice how to do it safely by role-playing the problem and coaching children to be respectful and caring with each other.

When children are having problems in how they interact with others, we have found that a very effective way to change their behavior is to practice with them what you want them to do and then coach them in the moment to use this behavior in real life. For example, you might say to a young child, modeling the very respectful tone of voice, attitude, and words you want her to use. "Instead of saying, "MINE", you can ask for what you want in a kind way. Please say, "Please wait. You can use this when I'm done!"

Insist that the child repeats the statement in a kinder way. For more about this approach, see *Practice as a Management Tool for Unsafe, Disrespectful Behavior* in the Appendix. You may need to wait until your child has calmed down enough to listen and join you in your practice.

How can I protect my children from getting lost?

Being lost is traumatic for a child, and having a lost child is very traumatic for parents. First of all, try to prevent children from getting lost by doing your best to make sure you stay fully aware of where they are when you are out in public. It's easy to become distracted by talking with someone or looking at someone.

Remember that a small child is not truly with you when you are at a store or other busy public place unless you are holding onto that child or that child is holding onto you. Next, have a Safety Plan in case a child does get lost. As soon as children can understand, each time you go into a busy public place, ask, "What's our Safety Plan if we get lost?"

Children can practice how to NOT leave the public area, to go to the check-out counter, interrupt a busy adult, and ask for help. They can learn to ask a mother with small children for help. At larger group activities designed for small children, parents sometimes write their cell phone numbers on their children's arms just in case they get lost in the crowd.

Creating Little Books And Little Signs For Little People

Understanding their world helps everyone to feel safe, especially young children. Toddlers and preschoolers tend to be literal and to live in the 'here and now.' Changes that seem normal to adults can be frightening and confusing to young children because they don't understand what is going on and what is going to happen. Verbal explanations are often not enough to take an idea that is theoretical and make it real in a concrete way.

During her leadership of the Parent-Toddler groups at the Early Childhood Center of Cedars Sinai Hospital in Los Angeles, a licensed clinical social worker named Phyllis Rothman initiated the Little Book Project. The purpose of this project was to support parents in making little books to help prevent and resolve emotional problems for small children.

All you need is a few pieces of paper folded in half and stapled down the middle to make a book. You can make a plot that tells the story of what is going to happen or that explains something that has happened. Use stick figure drawings or photos with one sentence on each page following this plot:

- A neutral statement of the situation: "Darla likes to run down the sidewalk."

- The problem: "Darla's mom gets worried and upset."

- The solution: "Darla will Check First before she runs – and Wait at the corner."

- The happy ending: "Everyone is safe and has fun."

Here are a few sample plots. Keep it simple with just one or two ideas per page.

Mommy Goes On A Big Trip. Mommy has to go on a big trip for her work. Mommy kisses me and waves, "Bye-Bye." I don't want Mommy to go so I cry. Mommy is sad, too. She goes on an airplane. Mommy calls to talk on the phone. Mommy comes home. She is happy and gives me a big hug. I am happy to have Mommy home.

The Owie Book. I was riding my tricycle. I crashed down the hill. I got a big cut. There was red blood. I cried. The doctor gave me a shot. I cried some more. It hurt to clean out the dirt. I cried harder. My cut got better. I got to ride my trike but not down the hill.

I Go to Day Care. Daddy takes me to day care. I cry when he goes away. The teacher reads a story. We eat lunch. We take a nap. I play with my friends. Mommy comes and gives me a big hug. I am too busy and not ready to leave. Mommy waits and talks to the teacher. We go home.

The Too Busy Morning Story. I am sleepy when I get up and want to cuddle. Mommy and Daddy are in a big hurry because they are late. I don't want to get dressed and Daddy makes me. I spill my milk at breakfast. Mommy yells and cleans up. I cry and Mommy is sorry. Daddy says, "We are TOO BUSY!" We all give each other a big hug.

Children understand that books are important. Having their own book that tells their own story makes them feel important. According to Phyllis Rothman, "In my practice, I have seen children go from feeling helpless to feeling empowered when adults helped them understand a problem, express a feeling, or address a fear by making their own little books."

Using the same concept, Kidpower uses cartoons in our *Safety Comics* and curriculum books to help adults explain core safety skills to their children. Adults can then take these ideas and create their own little books to show young children how to apply these ideas to their own lives.

In addition, Kidpower has created the Safety Signs described in the Appendix to help everyone remember key personal safety concepts. Think of how often signs are posted to remind adults about what the safety rules are.

We constantly see traffic signs telling us the speed limit and reminding us that roads are slippery when wet. We see signs in bathrooms about washing our hands before returning to work and signs in parks about not littering and being careful with fire.

Children also can greatly benefit from signs to remind them about what they are supposed to do – and not do. One mother posted a little sign with a drawing of a child stopping and asking an adult before going out the door next to their front door with the words: CHECK FIRST. When this child's grandmother came to visit, this three-year old came to a screeching halt by the door and ran back inside to make sure it was okay to take her grandma outside to see the garden.

Puppetpower:
An Effective Method For
Getting And Keeping
Attention

Most children love stories. On hiking trips, my son Arend at a very young age used to walk cheerfully for endless miles, as long as his father or I kept telling him a story.

Even though Arend would otherwise be too tired, his little feet would fly along the trail unless we paused for a breath. Then he would beg, "Please keep telling the story." It didn't matter how silly the story was or whether or not it made any sense.

When adults pick up a puppet, doll, or stuffed animal to help act out the story, it usually works like magic.

Kidpower first developed Puppetpower because we started teaching hundreds of two- and three-year-old children in preschool programs. Although many of these children were not used to paying attention for more than a few minutes at a time, they would see a puppet and become instantly quiet because they anticipated a puppet show, which they thought of as being fun.

You can use puppets to show why safety skills are important and what the skills are. You can then coach children to copy what their toys were doing. Almost all Kidpower "People Safety" skills and ideas can be shown using puppets.

Puppet-teaching techniques

For teaching with puppets to work, adults need to be visible, vivid, clear about the point that they want to make, and connected with the children. Use puppets to help you to show and not just to tell. Sometimes puppets can get so caught up in entertaining the children that they take on a life of their own. Remember that the puppets' job is to help you to teach important skills and not just to play.

Anything can become a puppet. Once you start to move an object around, talk for it, and give it a personality, children will respond to it.

I used to make up stories at the dinner table, picking up anything handy to make a point or just for fun. For example, "Cup says to Spoon, 'Get out of my coffee!' Spoon says, 'But I just have to stir.' Cup says, 'Okay, but be quick about it.' Spoon sighs, 'Nag, nag, nag. You're always telling me what to do.'" From here, the story might go into a fantasy about Spoon running away and getting into lots of trouble, or model some form of conflict resolution.

Children are great at coming up with their own ideas. For example, a child might turn a big spoon and a small spoon into a Mommy Spoon and a Baby Spoon, and have the Baby Spoon fall down and get help from the Mommy Spoon.

Be sure that all the children watching you can see what you are doing. Adults sometimes accidentally block the visibility of smaller people because they don't realize that parts of their larger bodies or of other bodies are getting in the way.

With a group, being visible might mean standing up and/ or turning so that all children can see the action. If you are having a puppet do a practice with a human, be sure the human's face is also visible to everyone watching, rather than only looking at you. You might need to tell the human helping you demonstrate to sit or stand next to you instead of in front of you, so that everyone's faces are easy to see.

Once you animate a puppet, it can become real to young children with a life of its own. Be sure that any puppets or stuffed animals you use are treated with respect. Put them into their special bag or set them carefully next to you.

If you are going to teach with puppets to different groups of children, you might have special puppets that you keep in a special bag. Do not let children play with your puppets. It spreads germs and is too much of a distraction. Your puppets are your helpers, not their toys.

Simple puppets that you can take off and on your hands quickly and move easily work best. Puppets with arms are helpful for making Fences or Mean Word Catchers, but your puppets do not need legs to be effective.

- To show shock, have a puppet jerk backwards and gasp.

- To show domination when one puppet is acting mean or with a power imbalance when one puppet is an adult, raise your arm so that the adult or the mean-acting puppet is higher than the other puppet.

- To show family interactions, you can have puppets of different sizes of the same species (though this is not required: young children happily watch different animals and different size characters interacting together).

- To show cowering or sadness, turn the puppet's back to the other puppet, close its body down with its arms over its head, and shake.

- To make it cry, add sound effects in a play-acting way, such as crying, "Boo, hoo, hoo."

- To show fear, have the puppet jump and put its arms out and squeal, "Eek!"

- To show grumpiness, use the puppet's arms to scrunch up its face and name the feeling such as, "Duck is in a Bad Mood! See her Bad Mood Face?"

- To show pride, spread the puppet's arms out and move it a little, raising it a bit higher. Make a happy "Ahhhh" sound.

So your audience will know who is talking, look at the puppet that's talking. Have your face and tone of voice mirror what the puppet is feeling. Move the head or body of the puppet talking. Change your voice a little for the different characters, such as high pitched for Mouse, low pitched for Bear.

Just as with other role-plays, you have to set the stage so your audience will know what is going on, but this only takes a short sentence. You will lose children's attention if you tell the whole story verbally first and then use the puppets. Instead, just say one introductory sentence capturing where they are and what they're doing. Then, use the puppets to help you to act out the story.

In practices with very young children, have a puppet instead of a loved adult pretend to be intrusive, mean, or scary. Adults can then coach children to throw hurting words away, set boundaries, or yell and run to safety.

Once children are good at the skill and able to understand about pretending, adults can add realism by pretending to be a person who is acting in a way that is not safe.

Remember that we do not recommend encouraging children to act in ways that are hurtful or upsetting to each other, even if they are pretending.

To see free, short Puppetpower videos, visit the video section of the Kidpower online Library.

People Safety teaching stories and practices using puppets and other props

Below are demonstrations of core Kidpower skills adapted to the developing understanding of children as young as two or three years old.

The Real Trash Can Introduction. Even very young children can learn and use the Kidpower Trash Can Technique for staying safe from mean words. Start by demonstrating the skill with a real trash can, preferably one from the children's own environment.

Start by placing the trash can directly in front of you. In a big group, put the trash can on a chair so everyone can see it. I sometimes say, "The star of this part of Kidpower is the Trash Can!" By having the trash can take a bow, it also becomes like a puppet. (Just one word of warning: be sure to hold the trash can by the outside so that you don't get something icky on your hands and check how full it is before you have it take a bow.)

Take a piece of paper, crumple it up dramatically and throw it on the floor. Ask, "What is that?" Get children to answer, "Trash!"

Ask, "Does it belong on the floor?" Shake your head and answer with the children, "No!"

Ask, "Should I eat it?" Pick up the paper and put it close to your mouth. Shake your head and answer with the children, "No!" You can add other leading questions that can be answered 'yes' or 'no,' such as, "Should I play with something in the trash?" Or, "Could I get sick if I eat something from the trash?"

Ask, "Where does trash belong?" Point and answer with the children, "In the trash can!"

Now you can transition to the following story by saying, "That's what we do with trash you can see. There is also trash in the world that you cannot see, but you can feel it and hear it. Mean words are like trash: you can't see them in the air, but you can hear them and feel them.

The 'You Are Stupid' Story. This story shows how words can hurt and how you can protect yourself. Put a puppet, perhaps Bear and Mouse, on each hand.

Set the stage by saying, "Bear and Mouse are friends and they like to laugh. Here they are laughing and having fun together."

Have Bear and Mouse facing each other, close, laughing, "Ha! Ha! Ha!"

Ask children, "Does this look safe?" Nod your head and answer with them, "Yes!"

Say, "Suppose that Mouse is in a Bad Mood? See her Bad Mood Face?" Show Mouse with a scrunched up face. "Suppose that Mouse calls her friend Bear a mean word like 'Stupid!'" Gasp.

Now show Mouse getting higher than Bear and shouting at Bear, "You are stupid!" Have Bear gasp and collapse crying.

Leave the two puppets in this position while you ask the children, "Does this look safe?" Shake your head sorrowfully and answer with them, "No!" Turn back to your puppet helpers and say, "Watch what Bear can do!"

Mouse says, "You are stupid!"

Bear gasps and then catches the word "stupid" and throws it into the trash can that is conveniently nearby. Then Bear opens his body up and says proudly, "I am smart." Ask the children, "Does that look safe?" Smile and nod your head while you answer with them, "Yes!"

Now, have Mouse say, "You are stupid!" to the children. Coach children to practice using their hands as 'Mean Word Catchers' to catch the word 'stupid' and throw it in the trash. They can use their other hand to take the words "I am smart!" into their hearts as they say this out loud.

The 'I Don't Like You' Story. This story shows the problem with getting angry back at someone and how to protect yourself instead. Pick up Bear and Mouse again and say, "Let's suppose that Bear is in a bad mood this time." Show Bear's Bad Mood Face.

Mouse goes up to Bear and says cheerfully, "Bear, I want to play with you!"

Bear goes higher than Mouse and snaps, "I do not want to play with you! I don't like you!"

Mouse gasps and goes higher than Bear and shouts, "Well, I HATE you!"

Bear gasps and pushes Mouse, yelling, "I HATE you more!"

Ask children, "Does this look safe?" Shake your head sorrowfully and say with them, "No!" Turn back to your puppet helpers and say, "Watch what Mouse can do to be safe."

Mouse goes up to Bear and says cheerfully, "Bear, I want to play with you!"

Bear goes higher than Mouse and snarls, "I do not want to play with you! I don't like you!"

Mouse gasps but then catches the mean words in her paws and throws them into the trash can you have nearby. She then looks proud and says, "I like myself. I will find another friend to play with today!"

Ask children, "Does this look safer?" Smile and nod your head as you answer with them, "Yes." Now ask, "Who will play with Mouse?" Raise your own hand and most likely, the children with you will raise theirs.

At a play group or school you can add, "At our school, you can go and find another friend to play with you."

Coach children to practice using their Mean Word Catchers to catch and throw away the words, "I hate you. I don't want to play with you." Coach children to say aloud and to use their other hand to take into their hearts the words, "I love myself. I'll find another friend to play with today."

Next, you can use this as a transition to teaching the Kidpower Trash Can by saying, "If you don't have a real trash can handy, you can make a Kidpower Trash Can." Show children how to do this by putting a hand on one hip. The hole this makes is used as a trash can. They use the other hand to catch mean words and to take in nice words. With young children, you can practice by having Bear say things like, "You are bad!" Or, "You are mean!" They can catch these hurting words and then throw them away and say, "I am good!"

The Tickling Story. This story shows when touch is wanted, the problem when it is not wanted, and what to do about unwanted touch. Pick up Bear and Mouse again and say, "Now we are going to practice Safety with Touch. Bear and Mouse are tickling each other and having fun." Show the two puppets tickling each other.

Ask, "Does this look safe?" Smile, nod your head, and answer with the children, "Yes!"

Ask, "Suppose that Bear wants to tickle, but Mouse does not want to tickle right now."

Show Bear going, "Tickle, tickle, tickle." Show Mouse turning away from the tickling, and Bear continuing to tickle on top of a cowering Mouse.

Keep the two puppets in this position as you ask the children, "Does this look safe?" Shake your head and answer with the children, "No!" Now turn back to the puppets and say, "Watch what Mouse can do."

Bear starts to tickle and says, "Tickle, tickle, tickle."

Mouse moves back, makes a fence with her paws, and says firmly, "Stop! I don't like it!"

Bear moves back, sounds surprised, and says, "Oh, sorry."

Now have children practice stopping you tickling them. Do this without actually tickling them. Say, "Suppose I was going to tickle you." Wiggle your fingers towards children in a tickling motion and say, "Tickle, tickle, tickle." If you think that your pretending like this might be confusing, have Bear be the one who tries to tickle at first.

Coach children to practice what to say and do with you as you explain and show it. Say, "Put your hands out like a fence. Let me see your hands like a fence. Good, now say, 'Stop, I don't like it!'"

Finally, pretend to tickle and say again, "Tickle, tickle, tickle." Coach children to use their hands fences in front of them and say, "Stop! I don't like it!"

The Pulling Ear Story. This story shows how to deal with people whose feelings are hurt when you set boundaries. Pick up Bear and Mouse again and say, "Watch this. Suppose that Mouse is pulling Bear's ear." Show Mouse grabbing and pulling Bear's ear.

Show Bear yelling, "OW! OW!" Show Mouse giggling and pulling.

Keep your puppet helpers in this position as you turn to the children and ask, "Does this look safe?" Shake your head and answer with the children, "No!" Turn back to your puppet helpers and say, "Watch what Bear can do."

Mouse starts to pull Bear's ear. Bear pulls back, makes a fence, and says firmly, "Stop I don't like it!"

Mouse starts crying, "Boo, hoo, hoo. That hurt my feelings!" Show Mouse crumpling in sadness.

Keep the two puppets in this position as you turn to the children and say, "Oh dear! Look how sad Mouse is! If Mouse is sad because Bear didn't like it, did Bear do something wrong?"

Children are often not sure. They might say, "Bear hurt Mouse's feelings. It's not nice to hurt feelings." This is a wonderful opportunity to point out that, even if someone is unhappy, you can still tell him or her to stop hurting you.

Show the problem again. Have Mouse pulling Bear's ear. Ask, "Does this look safe?" Shake your head and answer with the children, "No!" Ask, "Does Bear have the right to tell Mouse to stop hurting him?" Nod your head and answer with the children, "Yes!"

Now say, "Mouse is hurting Bear, so Bear is going to tell Mouse to stop."

Again, Mouse pulls Bear's ear. Bear moves away, makes a fence with his paws, and says, "Stop! I don't like it!"

Mouse crumples in sadness and cries, "I am so sad! That hurt my feelings."

Bear says calmly and firmly, "I am sorry you are sad, and you still have to stop." For children who can say only a few words, Bear might just say, "Sorry, and STOP!"

Finally, coach children through the whole practice of stopping unwanted touch and of dealing with hurt feelings. Pretend to tickle. Pretend to cry. If children get stuck, tell them what to do and let them do it.

The Hitting Story. This story shows that some things are not a choice and that anything that bothers you should not have to be a secret. Use just Mouse for this story. Show Mouse about to hit a child sitting next to you and ask, "If Mouse was really angry and was going to hit someone, would it be okay for me to stop her?"

Nod your head and answer with the children, "Yes!" Explain, "That's right. I should stop Mouse because it is not safe to hit people. A grown-up needs to stop her if she cannot stop herself."

Show Mouse trying to hit the child next to you. Stop Mouse with your other hand and say, "No hitting, Mouse!"

Show Mouse pulling away, making a fence, and saying back at you, "Stop, I don't like it."

Tell Mouse, "I understand you don't like it. I have to stop you if you cannot stop yourself. Hitting is not safe."

Show Mouse saying angrily, "I'm going to tell on you!"

Turn to children and ask, "Is it okay for Mouse to tell?" Nod your head and answer with the children, "Yes!" Explain, "It is always okay to tell, because problems should not have to be a secret."

Turn back to Mouse, who again says, "I'm going to tell!"

Say to Mouse, "That's a good idea. Let's go tell together."

Explain to children, "Touch for health and safety is not always your choice, but it is always okay to tell. Problems should not be secrets."

The Copying Story. This role-play shows how to persist in setting a boundary and how to move away and get help if this doesn't work.

Do this role-play with a child and a puppet, perhaps Bear. Set the stage by saying, "Sometimes Bear here is a little bit rude and likes to pull kids' hair!" Have Bear gently pull the hair of your child helper. If the child has short hair, this could be changed to rubbing the child's head, pulling on the child's shoe, or gently poking the child's arm.

Coach the child to push Bear's paw away, to make a fence, and to say, "Stop! I don't like it!"

Act this out with Bear as you say, "Suppose Bear goes like this, 'Stop I don't like it! Nah, nah, nah, nah!'" Use a bratty, mocking tone of voice.

Ask, "What is this called?" Children know and will answer, "Copying!"

Ask, "Is copying kind of mean?? Nod your head and answer with the children, "Yes!"

Have Bear pull the child's hair and copy again. Coach the child to push Bear's paw away, to make a fence, and to say again, "Stop! I don't like it!"

Have Bear be really bratty and say, "Stop. I don't like it! Nah, nah, nah!"

Coach the child to say, "That's not funny!"

Have Bear continue copy in an obnoxious way and say, "That's not funny! Nah, nah, nah!"

Pause and say, "This is a time when you might feel like saying or doing something mean back to Bear, right?" Nod your head and let child answer, "Yes."

Explain, "It is normal to want to say something mean back when someone is bothering you. But if you do, is this going to make the problem bigger or better? Say with the child, "Bigger."

Continue to explain as you show what to do by squeezing your own lips and walking your own fingers along your arm, "This is why we have Mouth Closed Power. Squeeze your lips together like this to stop yourself from saying anything. Because it's hard to use Mouth Closed Power for very long, you can then use your Walk Away Power. So when Bear is Rude, first you are going to use your Mouth Closed Power and then your Walk Away Power, and then you are going to tell your grown-up that Bear is being rude."

Go through the whole role-play from the beginning. When Bear keeps copying after the second time the child asks him to stop, coach the child to squeeze her or his lips shut, to walk away, and to tell an adult what the problem is. If there is another adult there, this adult can say, "Thank you for telling me. You did a good job. I'll talk to Bear."

You can show Bear being unhappy when the child walks away. For example, Bear might say, "Nah, Nah… Huh? Hey, where are you going?! But… But… She just up and left! (Sniff. Sniff.) Now I'm all alone. This is no fun!"

The Animal Strangers Story. This role play introduces strangers through animals and gives the child practice in following the Checking First rule.

Have a child helper and a stuffed toy dog. Set the stage by explaining, "We are going to practice checking first. Let's pretend that you are at the park with your grown-up. You are playing here in the sandbox." Have the child sit near you. Point to an adult helper or a toy representing the child's adult some distance away and say, "Here is your grown-up sitting on the park bench."

Move the toy dog slowly towards your sitting child helper and say, "Let's imagine that this is a cute, sweet little dog that you really want to pet."

Ask, "Is it safe to let an animal that you do not know well come close to you?" Shake your head and answer with the children, "No."

Coach the child to stand up as soon as the dog tries to come close, to move away without talking, and to go check with the grown-up on the park bench. You can do this by telling the child, "Your job is to use your Mouth Closed Power, Your Stand Up Power, your Walk Away Power, and your Checking First Power. Ask your grown-up, 'Can I play with the dog?'"

When the child acts this out, pause and give the child extra help if needed. Coach the grown-up to say, "Thank you for checking first. Let's go together.' The person pretending to be this child's grown-up could also be another child, or you, switching roles.

Act out having the child's adult ask the dog's owner, "Is it okay to pet your dog?"

As the dog's owner, say, "Yes, my dog is very gentle. But let's notice if she wants to be petted."

Have the 'dog' act like she wants to be petted. Her tail is wagging. She is trying to lick the child's hand.

Have the owner say, "Put the back of your hand out slowly and carefully to let her smell you first."

Most young children will very delightedly let the 'dog' smell their hands and then pet the dog gently.

In places where children might encounter lots of dogs, you can add another practice. Have the dog act like she doesn't want to be petted or is a little too wild to be safe to pet. This can get children in the habit of noticing the dog's behavior instead of just listening automatically to what the owner says.

Now, do another practice with a different child or with the same child if you are practicing with just the two of you. Again, imagine being in the park with the child playing and the child's adult on the park bench. Use a stuffed toy that could be a wild animal that is not something that often attacks people, such as a bird, a squirrel, or a rabbit.

Say, "Pretend this is a real wild bird." Have the bird hop towards the child, going "Chirp! Chirp!" Explain, "This bird wants to come close to you. Even if it is a very cute little bird, is it safe to play with an animal you do not know well?" Shake your head and answer with the children, "No!"

Coach the child to again stand up, move away, and Check First with her or his adult by asking, "Can I play with the bird?"

Coach the child's adult to say, "Thank you for Checking First. It's a wild animal, and I don't want you to touch it, but we can look at it together." Have the child and the adult admire the cute hopping bird.

You can now transition to introducing Stranger Safety by explaining, "The safety rules for people who are strangers is the same as for animals that you do not know well. Most are good but as soon as you notice them, move to your adult and Check First." Sometimes we show children a poster full of photos of happy-looking people who are all strangers to remind them that strangers can look like anybody.

The Using Awareness and Yelling Story. This example shows why awareness is important and how it works. Use any two puppets for this story. One is the aggressor and one is the victim. For right now, let's go back to our friends Bear and Mouse. Set the stage by saying, "Bear and Mouse are usually friends, but today Bear is acting a little scary."

Place Bear much higher than Mouse and have Bear growl, "Grrr!"

Explain, "Let's pretend that Mouse is scared." Have Mouse shaking to show fear. Say, "Suppose Mouse tries to pretend that Bear is not there." Hold the shaking Mouse so her back is to Bear.

Hold the two puppets where children can see, with Bear growling and Mouse with her back turned, shaking. Explain, "Mouse is wishing that Bear would go away. Is wishing working?" Shake your head with the children and say, "No."

Add, "Let's all wish with Mouse." Pause and let everyone wish together. Ask again, "Is wishing making Bear go away?" Again, shake your head with the children and say, "No."

Explain, "If Mouse tries to pretend that Bear isn't there by not looking, watch what happens."

Have Bear sneak up on Mouse and scare her with a loud, "Grrr!"

Have Mouse leap up in fear and squeak, "Eek! Eek!"

Ask the children leading questions to help them understand the lesson. "Did Bear scare Mouse?" Nod your head and answer with the children, "Yes."

Ask, "Was that safe?" Shake your head and answer with the children, "No!"

Say, "Watch what Mouse can do."

Again, have Bear sneak up behind Mouse, who has her back to him. This time, have Mouse turn around, look at Bear, make a stop sign with her paws, and yell, "STOP!"

Have Bear pull back with a "Gasp!"

Have Mouse scurry to her adult and yell, "I need help!"

Have the adult say, "I will help you!"

Now, get the child or children standing. Have Bear go, "Grrr!" Coach the children to make a stop sign and yell, "STOP!" Next, coach them to run to an adult yelling, "I NEED HELP!" Coach the adult to say, "I will help you."

The Waiting And Interrupting Story. This story shows when you have to wait, when it is safer to interrupt, and how to be persistent in asking for help.

Use two puppets, stuffed animals, or dolls that are of the same species. One is the adult and one is the kid. If you don't have one larger and one smaller, then hold the 'adult' higher than the 'child'.

In workshops, I set the stage by saying, "Suppose that Baby Elephant is playing a game and she needs a toy that she can't find. Her Mama Elephant is busy, busy, busy!" I turn to the children and ask, "Do your parents ever get busy, busy, busy?" I nod my head and answer with them, "Yes."

I set the stage by explaining, "Let's imagine that Mama Elephant is on the computer (or in the kitchen) getting work done."

Baby Elephant interrupts Mama Elephant and says, "Mama, I can't find my toy. I want it! Please help me find it right now."

Mama Elephant gets grumpy and says, "I'm busy. Don't interrupt! You'll have to wait!"

Continuing my story, I say, "Baby Elephant knows that sometimes she has to wait when she wants something. A little later, Baby Elephant has to go to the bathroom. She sees a great big bee buzzing around the toilet seat. Baby Elephant is afraid of the bee because it might sting her."

I turn Mama Elephant's back to Baby Elephant and ask my students, "Is it okay for Baby Elephant to interrupt Mama Elephant to help her with the bee?"

Since many children are not sure, I explain, "You wait if you want something, but you interrupt and keep asking if you need help with a safety problem. Is having a bee buzzing by the toilet seat when you need to go potty a safety problem?? I nod my head and answer with the children, "Yes."

I show Baby Elephant interrupting Mama Elephant, saying, "Mama, I need to go to the toilet, and there's a bee."

Mama Elephant does not pay attention and says, "Mmm. Hmm. That's nice, honey!"

Holding my stuffed animal helpers in place, with Mama Elephant facing away while Baby Elephant is asking, I turn to the children and ask, "Is Mama Elephant listening?" I shake my head and answer with the children, "NO."

Baby Elephant persists and says, "Mama, please look at me. I need help."

Mama Elephant gets angry and says in an angry voice, "What now? I told you not to bother me when I'm busy. I have to get this done!" She turns away again.

I turn to the children and ask, "Do your grown-ups ever get grumpy and not hear what you say if you bother them while they are busy?" I nod my head and answer with the children, "Yes." I ask another leading question, "Is it safer for Baby Elephant to go back and face the bee alone if she thinks it's dangerous, or is it safer to keep asking for help?" We agree that it is safer to get help.

Baby Elephant explains, "But Mama, this is about my safety!"

Mama Elephant turns to Baby Elephant and says, "Your safety! What do you mean?"

Baby Elephant says, "I have to go to the toilet, and there's a bee buzzing around the seat."

"Oh my goodness!" Mama Elephant says as she hurries to the toilet and gently shoos the bee out the window with her trunk. "Why didn't you tell me?"

To the great satisfaction of the watching children, Baby Elephant says, "I already did."

To the mild disappointment of my audience, I do not show Baby Elephant actually using the toilet, but I do show Mama Elephant very kindly patting Baby Elephant with her trunk and saying, "I am glad you told me. You did the right thing to interrupt me, and I am sorry for getting mad at you."

Baby Elephant says, "Thanks, Mama."

I then transition to having children practice interrupting busy adults to tell them about a safety problem. Sometimes, with young children, I have the puppet or stuffed animal pretend to be the busy adult so that I can coach the child.

Answering "Why" Questions Without Giving Too Much Information

Earliest Teachable Moment

Anyone who spends much time with young children knows that the question "Why?"comes up constantly – whether the question is why rabbits can't fly, or why can't I stand on the table in the middle of dinner or why can't I show someone my penis or vagina if I feel like it or why do I have to ask my grown-ups first before I can talk to strangers?

Some "Why?"questions are easy to answer. Rabbits can't fly because they don't have wings. You can't stand on the table because we don't want you to step in our food and you might fall off.

As adults, we sometimes have the job of not answering every question in the way it was asked. Getting into details about some kinds of "Why?"questions can lead to putting pictures into children's minds that don't need to be there.

With younger children, questions about safety rules on touching or strangers are often best answered just by saying, "Because that's our safety rule." Kids know that adults and families have rules. For example, the adult gets to say when kids get to have cookies and when they don't or that kids have to go to bed at 8 p.m. rather than 9 p.m. The reason that adults get to decide what the rules are is because adults have the job of taking care of children and of keeping them safe.

Kids ask "Why?"questions about sexual play, nudity, and strangers in the same way that they question other rules. As adults, we know that the reason for the safety rules about the private parts of the body is because there is the potential for someone to get hurt physically and emotionally. As adults, we know that there are dangerous people who might kidnap and harm children. But we don't need to inflict this information on our children sooner than necessary.

Answers like "doing this is bad or dangerous" are likely to be confusing, upsetting, and lead to more questions. Children know that showing or touching their private areas is not inherently painful and might be interesting or pleasurable. And, most of the time, interactions with people children don't know are likely to be very positive.

A clearer answer is, "Because doing this is against our safety rules." Younger children do not always need to know the reasons why we have rules, but they do need to know that the rules are there to help keep them safe.

If a child asks why touching private areas is against the safety rules, adults can say, "The safety rules are to help keep you safe and it can be unsafe to let someone touch or look at the private parts of your body unless I say it's okay." If a child asks why again, adults can say, "Because that is our rule."

A child who keeps asking about safety issues might have heard or read something upsetting. Often, you can find out what your child is thinking by answering the "Why?"question with your own question, "What do you think?" The answer can tell you what kind of help or information this child needs.

If a persistent curious child wants more and more details about bad things that might happen, you can set a boundary by saying, "I don't want to talk about the bad things that might happen. I want to talk about how you can stay safe most of the time and how you can get help if you need to."

Too much information too soon about details of bad things that might happen can be overwhelming for a child. Our job as adults is to encourage our children to enjoy being kids, while giving them the tools they need to grow up as safely and happily as possible.

Making A Safety Plan
For Bathroom Accidents

At times, life can seem very difficult for children who are struggling to master social skills and also to be in charge of their bodies. Doing something seen as babyish and socially unacceptable like peeing in their pants can feel like a very upsetting emergency.

One mother wrote us about a traumatic experience that thankfully turned out well. "While having a birthday party for my son at a local recreation center, our four- year-old daughter disappeared for a good ten minutes. My husband was watching the kids while I left to check on the pizza. They all said she was there one minute, gone the next.

"When I walked back in the building, it was sheer panic. Everyone was looking for her. It turned out our little girl had had a potty accident. She'd been so excited that she peed in her pants and was then terribly embarrassed. She was unfamiliar with the building and went to hide in a dressing room in a part the store that no one was in. I cried when I found her. I was so terrified and so thankful she was safe!"

Kids and even adults might have bathroom accidents for a variety of reasons – sleeping very soundly; getting too caught up in play and forgetting to go; not feeling safe about the bathrooms available and waiting too long; having clothes that they can't get undone quickly; having a physical problem; or being startled in a way that causes them to lose control. Dealing with the embarrassment of having a bathroom accident can make people miserable and even cause them to take actions that might put them into danger.

Here are six steps to developing a safety plan for bathroom accidents:

Make sure your children know what you want them to do

As soon as they can understand, children need to be told very clearly, "Once in a while, kids and even grown-ups have a bathroom accident and pee or even poop in their clothes. They might feel very embarrassed. If this happens, you might feel like hiding or running away, but that's not safe. Remember that your safety is more important than your embarrassment. Your job is to get help from the adult in charge and NOT to leave without checking first. Having a bathroom accident does not mean that you are bad or that you are a baby – it just means that you had an accident. The adult in charge will help you get cleaned up and get new clothes."

Concern about bathroom accidents looms large for younger children. I once asked a group of seven-year-olds where they would wait if they were lost in a huge store. They all said that they would wait by the bathrooms, which were in the isolated back of the store. When I asked them why, they explained with perfect seven-year-old logic, "Because then, if you needed to GO, you'd be right there!"

Make it safe to go to the toilet in unfamiliar places

Many young children are very conservative about where they feel comfortable using the toilet. Without some help, they might try to avoid going until it's too late. Every time you go to a new place with younger children, discuss where the bathroom is and what to do if they need to go. Remind them that, although you'd like to make sure they get to the toilet on time, you will not be upset if they have an accident, as long as they tell you so that you can help them.

One kindergarten teacher had an interesting challenge because their school was under construction and the children were going to have to use portable chemical toilets for a few months. She did a bathroom drill to show her students how the toilet worked and what to do and not do. Everyone got to practice "flushing" the strange toilets until the strange became more familiar. This teacher also sent her students to go to the toilet in pairs. That way the other child could stand outside the door (instead of using the complicated lock) and go for help if necessary.

One little boy was terrified about using an outhouse while camping until his parents told him that this was Smokey the Bear's toilet. After that, he couldn't wait to go!

Make sure that the adults your children are with will be supportive

You need to know that the adults in charge of your children will be matter-of-fact, calm, kind, and protective if your child has a bathroom accident – and that your child will never be shamed or teased about this happening.

Teasing from children about bathroom accidents needs to be stopped with the same commitment as you would stop other bullying. The message we want children to have is that they do not need to be ashamed of their bodies or of themselves, even if they accidentally do something that is socially unacceptable.

Help children remember to go

Children tend to live more in the moment and be less able to plan ahead than adults. Even if a child says that she doesn't need to go, pay attention to her body language. If she is squeezing her legs together or holding herself, she might be so focused on the action that she has forgotten to pay attention to what her body is trying to tell her. You can gently insist, saying something like, "I need to go, so let's go try together!"

Make a plan for bed-wetting and other potential problems

Some children sleep so soundly that they might not be able get through the night without peeing in the bed until they are six or seven. Five percent of all children are not dry overnight at the age of ten. This is NOT something they can control, and it IS something almost everybody will eventually grow out of. If you have any concerns about your child's bed-wetting, make sure to discuss it with his or her doctor who will be able to assess if there are any potential underlying problems to address and offer solutions.

Children who are different from their peers for any reason need tools and language to deal with it. Nighttime diapers can save a lot of discomfort and laundry. Older children can gain a sense of power by learning how to use the washer and dryer themselves if need be.

You can normalize this problem instead of making it a source of shame with a simple explanation, such as, "You are a very sound sleeper and your body doesn't wake up in time to go. This is something that happens to lots of kids and you will grow out of it when your body is ready."

If you are away from home, carrying an extra set of clothing just in case a child gets wet or dirty can prevent a lot of trouble.

Help your children understand that being embarrassed is something that happens to everybody.

Feeling alone and ashamed is destructive to a child's well-being and joy in life. Give children room to talk about their feelings, but don't be surprised if they don't want to. For younger children, you might act out stories about bathroom accidents with their toys.

Children of any age love hearing stories about their parents being kids. It's reassuring to hear that their parents or other important adults once peed in their pants, threw up all over someone, or got a thorn in their bottoms – and were very embarrassed, but were still able to feel good about themselves.

If you think a child might be feeling embarrassed and unable to talk about it, tell stories of times when you were embarrassed. If need be, make up happy endings that give your children the message that we don't have to be perfect to be great.

Pay attention to themes in your child's play that could give you clues about problems – is Teddy being called "Stupid" for having a bathroom accident? This can give you an opportunity to join in play with your child to have a happy ending for Teddy rather than directly talking to the child about the problem.

Managing Aggressive Behavior And Preventing Meltdowns

Parents, teachers, and caregivers of young children often come to Kidpower for help when their kids have trouble being safe with their bodies and their words.

"My three-year-old daughter can be so sweet one moment and then explode in a flash. Yesterday she deliberately destroyed a sand castle and then threw sand into the eyes of one of her friends in our playgroup."

"My son used to be so mellow but ever since he started kindergarten he's been copying another boy and hitting other kids."

"A girl in my first grade classroom melts down when she doesn't get her way and starts pinching, pushing, and sobbing uncontrollably."

"A boy in my day care center hates to come in from the playground. He'll throw himself onto the ground in a full-blown tantrum, flailing, wailing, and shrieking."

Some kids just come into the world expressing their feelings in a bigger way than other kids. They are filled with big joy, big fear, big excitement, and big anger – and these feelings can shift in an instant. This behavior needs to be managed for everyone's safety, but these big feelings are not because their parents did anything wrong.

As exhausting and frustrating as this can be, staying calm, loving, and firm while stopping children when they are acting out in ways that are potentially harmful is essential for parents and other caregivers.

Children who have lost control are likely to feel emotionally unsafe and may be physically unsafe if they are not stopped. Other children who see a child who is acting in a way that seems dangerous are also likely to feel unsafe unless an adult is taking charge of the situation in an effective and caring way. They might also start experimenting with imitating the behavior of the aggressive child.

Although aggressive behavior cannot be allowed to continue, adults must do this in a nondestructive way. Great harm can be done if an adult restrains an upset child in a way that is physically unsafe for the child or for the adult; acts worried or angry about the child being upset; or shames the child for losing control. Firm, kind, matter-of-fact adult intervention is necessary for everyone's emotional and physical safety.

Although the following seven strategies were written to help adults with younger children, most of them can also be adapted for intervening when older children struggle with aggressive behavior.

Be prepared that children will sometimes have difficulty staying in charge of their behavior

Children's brains are developing, and they don't have the same ability to control themselves that adults do. As soon as they can understand, it is important to begin teaching children skills for staying in change of their behavior while understanding that they need our supervision to stay safe and ongoing guidance to learn how to act safely.

Often, children with strong leadership qualities seem to need to define their boundaries by pushing against the boundaries of others and by experimenting with negative uses of their power.

With positive adult guidance, most of them grow up to be caring, respectful people.

Children who are highly sensitive sometimes act in ways that are not as "easy" or "standard" and often need adult support to learn behaviors that other children may learn more easily. Some people who recall intense episodes of strong feelings in childhood later become gifted writers, visionary leaders, or imaginative inventors as adults.

When children experience strong feelings, they need their adults to invest time, patience, effort, and compassion to help them learn how to handle these feelings constructively.

When children become overwhelmed, they might close down, tune out, become crushed with sorrow, or lash out verbally or physically.

Be realistic and honest instead of denying that there is a problem. Too often, people ignore out-of-control behavior as being normal until it escalates in a destructive way. Condemning a child who acts aggressively for being "bad" is also unhelpful. Aggressive behaviors do not mean that the children are bad or that either their parents or their teachers are incompetent. Meltdowns just mean that everyone involved needs support and skills in managing feelings before they reach the explosion point, in coping with overwhelm, and in controlling behavior so that everyone stays emotionally and physically safe.

However, learning how to release upset energy and strong feelings in a safe way is often necessary for people at any age. It can be very healthy for a child to have a big long cry or yell loudly after becoming intensely frustrated, emotionally hurt, or scared. Although children may need support in doing so in a way that does not hurt themselves or other, being allowed to release energy and feelings can help them to move on and find their equilibrium again. However, letting out feelings by acting with intentional or unsafe aggression is not the same and should be treated differently.

A useful book with drawings for helping adults under-stand and be able to explain to children how their brain works is *The Whole Brain Child: 12 Revolutionary Strategies to Nurture Your Child's Developing Mind* by Daniel J. Siegel, M.D. and Tina Payne Bryson, Ph.D.

Identify and reduce causes of stress that trigger outbursts

Understanding the "how" and "why of outbursts is important in finding positive solutions. Although the problem behavior can seem like a sudden explosion of feelings for no apparent reason, often there are patterns of when it is more or less likely to happen and some "lead up" time before the incident occurs.

Even though this is time-consuming, taking a week or more to write down all observations about when and how a child gets upset often will provide insights into changes, which might help to reduce the outbursts.

Document the behavior and see if any patterns emerge about what is different on the "good" days and the "hard" days. Does anything stand out? Here are some very common triggers to consider:

Transitions. Even if doing lots of different things is very fun, too much change can lead to children becoming over-stimulated. Many kids have far fewer outbursts when they have a calm, predictable schedule that includes time to play alone in their own space and regular special one-on-one time with their adults.

Sometimes a simple change of plan for a while can make a world of difference. For example, if your toddler throws tantrums in the store, consider making arrangements to handle shopping without her for few weeks.

Make leaving a favorite activity fun rather than stressful. If your child gets upset about leaving the park, agree on a plan before going to the park about how and when you are going to get ready to leave and give him lots of reminders about how much time is left. When it's time to go, stay cheerful even if your child is unhappy, give him something to look forward to about what's going to happen next, and tell a story about a favorite character that does silly things in order to be able to stay at the park all night long.

For many children, starting kindergarten or preschool can be a difficult transition. A child might start to struggle with power and control issues in an attempt to man-age a new environment. If your child is having a hard time, try to volunteer in the classroom both to help support the teacher and to understand more about the context of the problem.

If this is not possible, arrange to meet with your child's teacher to consider together how your child can be supported with this problem. Remember that even young children might also have ideas about what could help. If you can talk about the problem in a calm, non-blaming way with children, they may surprise you with the solution they generate. Even if their solution is not practical, they have been given a clear message that they have something valuable to contribute to overcoming this problem.

Even positive changes such as a new sibling, a new home, or a birthday party are often stressful to a young child. Of course, negative changes such as a divorce, a parent losing a job, or a death are likely to be hard on the whole family and to require extra support.

Too hot or too cold. Some children can be highly affected by temperature. When they are even a little too hot or too cold, they are more likely to get upset — and they often do not remember (as they get focused) to take on or off their jackets or get a drink of water. Practicing making sure their bodies are comfortable is very helpful so they will remember in the moment.

Needing more sleep. Some children need a very strict bedtime and wake up routine to get enough sleep —some children just need more sleep and when you are interested in learning everything you can about the world (like many five-year-olds!) it can be hard to get enough sleep. Some children need to start napping again for a while when they start new activities, such as taking a trip or going to a new school. Change is a big stress even when it is positive and having extra sleep can help kids with the transition.

Needing more physical adult contact. Some children seem to need a lot of "cuddle" time to help their bodies to calm. Sitting and reading interesting books, playing games (while sitting in an adult's lap) or being carried or held can be helpful.

Needing more physical activity. Some children need to move A LOT! In fact, moving can help them focus and integrate what they are learning. Being forced to sit still and pay attention for long periods of time can be extremely stressful for them.

Needing more space. Some children get overwhelmed when they get crowded by others. This is why so many difficulties at school happen in transitions — in line going to lunch, circle time, etc. Children often seem to bunch themselves together as they get more agitated, rather than giving themselves more space.

Have kids practice moving to the end of the line or the edge of the circle if they need space or calmly asking for some room. Have them practice stepping back and measuring with one arm to give lots of space in line rather than crowding forward. We tell kids it is more important to be safe in line, than first in line (something very important to many younger kids – and adults too). Help a child plan how to get space at the lunch table or when sitting in circle. Talk to your child's teacher about this if you think this is an issue and have him/her help you with a plan that would allow the child to move to a less crowded spot in a way that isn't too distracting to the class.

Over-stimulation. Less is usually more in preventing meltdowns. Try changing your schedule and structuring your day and space so that children are doing less, having fewer toys or games out at the same time, and slowing down.

Reduce or eliminate access to television or other technology so kids use their time doing imaginary play and being creative. If a child complains about being bored, don't rush to fix it. Encourage the child to figure out interesting things to do on her or his own for a while and then make a plan to have your undivided attention at a time that works well for both of you.

Hunger. Not having enough healthy food to eat can also lead to a child being more likely to get triggered. Children get so busy, they can forget to eat, and then don't realize how hungry they are. Or they fill up on junk food that doesn't really nourish their bodies. Making a plan to make sure kids eat healthy food right before school, at recess, at lunch, and right after school can help.

Medical or psychological issues. If other triggers don't seem to be relevant, a child who has a very low threshold for frustration and who is easily triggered in ways that become destructive or who shuts down suddenly should be assessed for an underlying medical, psychological, or neurological problem. Some children's behavior has improved dramatically because of not being constantly irritated by an allergy or another medical issue, or because the source of the problem was figured out and addressed.

Even if a child is not acting aggressively, checking for potential underlying problems is important anytime a child seems to struggle without an obvious reason why. For example, my daughter at age eight was having terrible trouble learning to read. No problem showed up on her regular check-up but, when I mentioned my concern to my own eye doctor in casual conversation, he checked her eyes out. She didn't have a vision problem but she did have a neurological delay with how her eyes tracked together. Her relief at having a reason why she was having more trouble than her classmates was enormous. And, after a few months of adaptive physical education, she started to read easily and joyfully.

Once you have identified possible triggers, experiment by making a change and seeing if it helps. Try slowing down the day, increasing physical activities, reducing stimulation, an extra snack, a long bath, cuddle and story time before bed, controlling body temperature, etc. Minimizing triggers is unlikely to stop all explosive behavior, but it can help children to have the best chance to prevent and control this behavior.

Teach children how to recognize and manage the feelings and actions that lead to unsafe behavior

Discuss what is going on to help the child understand. One mother named her child's explosive behavior as having "fast feelings" which is a caring, non-judgmental name to describe what happens when you suddenly get very upset and say or do hurtful things. Acknowledge that feeling angry and frustrated is normal but that we have to learn how to feel our feelings while staying safe with our bodies. Tell stories about times when you felt angry and hit or kicked. Discuss characters in books that make these kinds of mistakes. Act out situations with toys to show the problem and safe solutions. Make little books about the behavior the child is working on.

Teach kids skills for stopping aggressive behavior in the moment. Provide ways to use aggressive energy safely. All children benefit from having opportunities to be successful in being active and learning new things while staying emotionally and physically safe and in control of what they say and do. Yoga, for example, can be a fun way for children to practice getting centered using their bodies in strong, peaceful ways. So can the right kind of martial arts program.

When the child is calm, practice Kidpower skills as a fun and interesting way to be safe with people. Even children as young as two have been successful in learning and using these skills.

Picture books about these issues such as these two can be very helpful:

- *When Sofie Get's Angry – Really, Really Angry*: http://bit.ly/16vJKx9

- *Peaceful Piggy Meditation*: http://bit.ly/1biEOJn

Calm Down Power. To help a child stop himself from being upset. Practice by having him pretend to be upset and then breathing slowly and deeply in and out, squeezing the palms of his hands together, and straightening his back. Remind him to use his Calm Down Power when he starts to get upset by coaching him through these motions and then congratulate him when he manages to do this even partially.

Mouth Closed Power. To help a child stop herself from saying hurtful or inappropriate things, biting, or being unsafe in other ways with her mouth. Younger children might need to practice by pushing their lips together AND putting their hands over their mouths to help them to stop. You can rehearse by going over a situation that happened (i.e. being rude about another child being "stinky") and having her get ready to say something mean and then stop. You can then come up with other situations. Do it multiple times a day at first. Reward her for practicing - a big hug, hi five, saying how proud you are, are all ways to make her feel good about learning.

Hands Down Hands Together Power. To help a child learn to stop himself from hitting or hurting others. This can be done by pressing his hands down at his sides and grabbing his pants, holding his own hands, or putting them into his pockets so they are hard to get out. This gives his hands something else to do – and also lets him feel his own strength.

This can be done by pressing his hands down at his sides or putting them into his pockets so they are hard to get out. Role-play situations. Then have a cue —when you say "Hands Down", his hands go to his sides and grab his pants or into his pockets. When you say, "Hands Together", he clasps his hands together. Reward him for being safe with his hands —you may find an actual reward chart is helpful with this —with small tangible rewards that you phase out as he gets better at self-control.

Move Away Power. To help a child move herself to a quiet place where she can calm down or to a grown-up who can help her. Make a quiet space for her at home, school, etc. where she can go and take a breath or two, jump up and down, hug a pillow, whatever helps her to calm down but is away from kids she may hurt. Her adults need to be able to come and check in with her quickly if she moves to this space so they can provide support if she needs it.

Walk Away Power. To practice walking away from trouble quickly before it gets bigger. Practice by pretending to be a kid who is about to push or poke, without actually doing this to the child. Coach the child to leave with an attitude that is aware, calm, respectful, and confident.

Use practice as a natural consequence of making unsafe choices. You don't want to make kids who have problems acting safely feel bad, but it is important they see the consequences of destructive behavior. Stop a child from being aggressive immediately and firmly, with loving support and simple clear language. "When you hit me, it hurts. I feel sad. Do not hit me. I love you very much. You are a good person. Let's practice stopping yourself from hitting."

Try to use the same simple language each time. If a child hits or hurts someone, the consequence can be to practice stopping, acknowledge the feelings that led to the out-burst, review the "plan" on using safe ways to manage aggressive feelings, and then practice the plan together.

Create a plan for how to prevent and handle outbursts for every place the child might be

If you have children who need help with anger management, anticipate potential problems and make a plan. Teaching them how to calm themselves down when they feel upset is a skill that will serve kids their whole lives.

Children are different. What works well in helping one child to handle intense feelings may be different for an-other child. Here are some specific suggestions from a Head Start and Kindergarten teacher whose students who struggled with being safe with their bodies and their words.

Create a family plan for how to handle outbursts. You may need a few of them (one for when he feels very sad, one when she feels frustrated, etc.) or, maybe even more specific ones (how to handle someone taking your toy, how to handle someone saying something that hurts your feelings, etc.).

Describe the situation with each step that happens and that you want to have happen. Help your child make a new plan by breaking things down. For example, start with a story about what actually happens: **1)** Lara feels angry, **2)** Lara hits, **3)** Friend gets hurt.

Now, create a new story with the steps you want to happen: **1)** Lara starts to feel angry, **2)** Lara takes two big breaths, **3)** Lara puts her hands down, **4)** Lara gets help from her mom/dad/teacher/etc., **5)** Adult helps, **6)** Lara feels better, **7)** Friend is happy too. You may need to make the steps VERY simple at first, but write them down on a big piece of paper with pictures, or as a little book with drawings, or on big flashcards.

Give in-the-moment coaching. When a problem starts to come up, coach your child to follow his plan. At first, you may only be able to talk about it with him and then go through the plan after the situation is over and he has calmed down, but over time he may be able to stop and follow his plan in the moment.

Spend time working on the pieces of the plan, especially the parts on how to calm down. Help your child to identify her feelings when they are happening or after-ward when she can remember. For example, she can say I feel "hot" or "sad." Draw a picture of the feeling or make a physical movement for the feeling (sad could be making a sad face or putting your finger on your cheek, hot could be waving your arm by your face). Have her make the movement if she can say the feeling when she is feeling it. The more she (and you) can focus in on the feelings she is getting as soon as they happen, the better able you will both be in helping to re-direct the feelings.

Be prepared to manage bossiness. Sometimes kids who have trouble with control start "policing" other kids and even adults. While this can feel annoying, it also is pretty normal that children who are struggling with the rules themselves feel a need to tell everyone else about the rules. It can be a way they are processing the rules, or it can be to show that others don't always follow the rules themselves or it can be part of their personalities. What often works best is just to say, "You are responsible for you and ___ is responsible for himself. You follow the rules for yourself and let him follow the rules for himself. If you see someone doing something unsafe, tell me."

A Success Story Using These Skills and Strategies to Make a Plan for Upsets. For example, one boy, who we'll call Sam, was having trouble when he started kindergarten.

Sam learned to identify how he was feeling right before he got upset (even though his outbursts before had seemed to happen abruptly). With his parents and teacher, he developed a cue where he would say how his internal thermostat was. Sam wanted to feel just right. He would put his finger against his chest: to the left was too cold, he was feeling sad; to the right, too hot, angry: and in the middle was just right.

Once he had identified his feelings, Sam learned how to do something about what he was feeling so he could get to the middle. If he was too hot, sometimes cooling down meant going with an aide to run around the field or he would get a drink of water and jump up and down twenty times to get out his energy. If he was feeling too cold, warming up could mean getting a cuddle from his teacher, holding her hand for a few minutes, or holding a stuffed animal.

Sam also worked on breathing in the moment, holding his own hands so he wouldn't hit with them, and moving away to a quiet space where he had some room so he could be safer with his body. He started to have more fun and fewer problems at school.

Understand and stay in charge of your own emotional triggers

We want our children to be happy. However, our job as adults is not to keep children happy all the time, but to keep them safe and help them learn and grow. Even though we know this intellectually, it can be hard not to take personally the negative things an upset or defiant child might say or do.

If you find yourself getting triggered by a child's behavior, remember that, before you can be emotionally and physically safe in managing this child, you must be completely in charge of your own feelings. Children are very sensitive to adults who project ambivalence, repressed resentment, or guilt. If need be, put your unhappy feeling aside to deal with later and focus on being compassionate with the child's point of view while setting the necessary boundaries on behavior.

If you find yourself having a hard time with a specific child's behavior, address your own feelings instead of wishing they would go away. Often just talking about your frustration or irritation privately with another adult can be enough to help you gain more perspective.

If you feel that you cannot cope with your child's behavior, consider getting professional help sooner rather than later. If a child's behavior is causing exhaustion and conflict, sometimes a few sessions of play therapy or family therapy can give everyone tools for turning difficult behavior into an opportunity to grow.

Be a powerful, respectful adult leader when taking charge of an out-of-control child

Children need to be stopped from dangerous or destructive behavior. They also need to see adults taking charge of safety in ways that are calm, respectful, and firm.

Having feelings of frustration, anger, fear, and embarrassment can be normal when kids are acting out. However, if adults act in shaming or hurtful ways towards kids who are behaving unsafely, they are showing kids exactly the opposite behavior of what these kids need to learn about how to handle feeling upset. Instead, show kids that, no matter what you might be feeling inside, you are staying in charge of what you say and do because their well-being is important to you.

So, take a breath and get calm before you react.

Prevent problems by staying close to a child who has trouble being safe with her or his body and words so that you can intervene quickly, before the behavior starts to escalate. Be prepared to step in quickly and safely both verbally and physically by:

Earliest Teachable Moment

- Using simple words in a firm, directive voice, without screaming at the child, say, "Put that down!" "No biting!" "No hitting!"

- Staying close enough that you can easily take away a toy that is about to be thrown or stop a child's hand from hitting another child.

- Moving to sit or stand in between two kids who are having trouble being safe with each other.

Some children will hear a stage whisper better than a loud voice. In an emergency, though, if a child is about to be hurt, be prepared to be forceful. If a child is about to run into the street, shout, "STOP!" and grab the child's hand if need be.

If a child throws a complete tantrum, do your best to help the child to regain control while keeping everyone safe until this happens. Kids who have lost control usually need both physical space and emotional reassurance. Make sure the child is in a safe place and not about to get hurt or hurt anyone else. Stop the child from doing something dangerous.

Even if a child does not understand the words, you can talk to him in a calm reassuring voice, saying things such as, "I am right here. I'm going to help everyone stay safe right now." The message needs to be, "I care about you!" – NOT, "You are a bad child."

Once the child is able to respond, give simple clear directions in a warm voice to help her get centered and to communicate caring. "Here's a tissue so you can blow your nose. Here's a little drink of water. Let's go to the bathroom and wash your face."

If a child is able to understand, after everything is calmed down, you can discuss what happened and how to prevent getting so upset again. Never mention in any derogatory fashion what happened during the outburst. Instead, you can tell stories, practice skills, and make plans as described above.

Don't contain a child physically unless this is a child you normally hold and you are emotionally centered yourself. Even if this is your own child, be sure you are being firm but gentle in how you hold the child so that you are keeping the child's body safe without squeezing or hurting. If you need to be physically close to a child who is having a tantrum, protect your own body by staying out of the way of head butts and flailing arms and legs.

For caregivers and teachers: If you are responsible for other people's children, make a plan and get permission

Agree ahead of time with the parents and/or your supervisor about how to handle behavior problems and what you are and are not authorized to do.

Remember the Kidpower boundary principles that *Problems Should Not Be Secrets and to Keep Asking Until You Get Help.* If a child in your care acts destructively, tell the parents and your supervisor right away what happened.

- Notice problems when they are small, before they reach the explosion point. Work together with other staff, parents, and, if possible, the child to make a plan for stopping trouble sooner rather than later.

- Use your awareness to notice potential danger signals and intervene by re-directing the child firmly and kindly into a different activity whenever possible. Instead of lecturing about what the child mustn't do and why, focus on what the child CAN do by offering acceptable choices with enthusiasm.

- Have a plan for keeping the other children safe while you are caring for the child who needs help.

Different people in a program are likely to have different levels of experience and training, so it makes sense that they will have different levels of permission. Before you are left in charge of children, make sure you know what the rules are about restraining children in your care if they need to be stopped from destructive or defiant behavior.

Make sure your center or school has a plan that is clear about who has permission to do what if a child melts down in a way that is potentially unsafe and that spells out exactly what to do. What kinds of prevention tools are available to you? What are you expected to do to keep the children safe in the moment if a child has a meltdown? Who do you call for help? How do you call for help? What if that person isn't there? How do you report what happened?

Learning to handle aggression safely can become a chance to grow

Children need to understand that all of their feelings are acceptable and normal, including anger. Everyone gets upset sometimes and wants to do hurtful things. As adults, we can help our kids learn how to stay in charge of what they say and do even if they are feeling very angry or upset at that moment. Being able to recognize when you are feeling upset, take care of your feelings in positive ways, and act safely no matter how you feel inside are tremendous life skills!

Born To Be Free: Coping With Kids Who Wander, Climb, And Hide

Earliest Teachable Moment

I will never forget when our four-year-old son Arend disappeared in a clothing store. One second he was there, and the next he was gone! We searched everywhere and were about to call the police when we suddenly saw his little shoes on the floor sticking out below the rack of men's shirts. He had squeezed in there to explore and was entertained when all the adults were calling for him.

Another time, Arend shimmied up the flagpole at his sister's school, far out of my reach. "Come down!" I said firmly. "You are up too high."

"No I'm not!" my son explained nonchalantly. "I can even hold on with just my legs." To my horror, he let go with his hands to show me, squeezing his legs tightly around the pole.

"You are up too high for ME!" I said again, doing my best to sound calm. "Please come down right now!" "Oh all right!" my son sighed and slipped safely down the flagpole.

The overwhelming terror when your child disappears or abruptly becomes dangerously out of your reach can be heart stopping. We see the potential hazards but most young children don't see the world the same way we do. And our priorities are different. Their safety and well-being are the most important things in our lives. Unless they have learned differently, acting on their impulses is usually what is most important to them in the moment.

Kids are not doing this because they are bad or are trying to make our lives miserable. They are motivated because they want to head to a favorite place, get caught up in the joy of running or exploring, see something interesting, or want to escape an upsetting situation.

Taking care of our feelings

Some children are even bigger wanderers, higher climbers, and more determined hiders than others. Almost always, this is because they were born that way rather than because of anything their parents did or did not do. These children often need large wide-open spaces that many families are not in a position to provide. As one father told me, "If we could live on a farm and my son's teachers could run or jump or do cartwheels next to him and teach him at the same time, that would be ideal." We can look for safe opportunities for our kids to run free – and, the rest of the time, we need creativity, patience, and persistence to cope with these children's huge drive to explore and keep moving.

Comparing our children with other children who sit calmly and learn easily is just going to make us feel bad without being helpful. Instead, we can accept that a child who comes into the world with tremendous energy and a body that can't seem to stop moving requires a bigger space and perhaps more need for repetition and practice than other kids. We can relieve frustration in the moment by taking deep breaths and giving ourselves permission to think, "THIS IS FRUSTRATING!" We can get respite from parenting by taking breaks where others we trust take care of our child. We can connect with other parents who understand or, if need be, get professional help, to gain perspective, refocus, and recognize and stop triggered thinking when it happens. "He just does it to be bad" or "She's been difficult since she was born" are examples of triggered thinking.

Concrete simple rules and skills to stay safe

Because young children tend to think in concrete, literal terms, they need consistent definitions and ongoing practice of concrete, specific safety rules and skills to help them develop an understanding about how we want them to act in different situations.

"See the boundary", "Wait", "Check First", "Stop", "Turn around", and "Stay Together" are concepts and skills that can help to prevent wandering, climbing, and hiding.

You can help your child to develop safety habits for using these skills by:

- Defining physical boundaries and the rules that go with these boundaries as concretely and consistently such as the door, the room, the house, the sidewalk, the driveway, the yard, and the street.

- Teaching safety skills as soon as possible.

- Practicing and rehearsing the skills and reinforcing the boundaries by role-playing common problems.

- Reviewing the plan using the skills before you go anywhere.

- Providing constant reminders of when to use these skills with rewards for doing so.

One common problem is that family members, teachers, and other caregivers will often use highly varying words and ideas to explain about safety, which can be confusing for anyone who is learning something new or changing unsafe habits, especially young children.

Our *Kidpower Safety Signs* that are in the Appendix were originally created as a tool for showing core safety concepts in a very simple form for people with limited speech. These Safety Signs create a common language that makes it easy and fun for everyone, everywhere, to use the same words, gestures, and ideas about staying safe with people.

These concepts and skills can also be taught with Little Books and puppets as described above.

Learning how to "Wait"

Remembering to "Wait" can keep your child from leaving a place unexpectedly. To teach how to "Wait", you can use any concrete symbol that makes where your child needs to "wait" very clear, including:

- Red tape across doors or floors.

- A big red Wait or Stop Sign by the door.

- Making a "No Circle" – a circle with a diagonal line through it – for anywhere that it is not okay to go without holding a known adult's hand –the front door, the classroom door, the back yard gate, etc.

Learning how to "Stay Together" and to "Check First"

When a child knows to "Stay Together" with you, getting separated through wandering becomes far less likely. To teach how to "Stay Together" when you go out, you can:

- Make a plan that you are going to "Stay Together" before you leave and review each time before you go out.

- Play games where you move in different directions and your child sticks to your side like glue.

- Teach the Kidpower Safety Sign for "Stay Together" or create your own sign and practice using with examples of places where temptations might be likely such as the mall or Farmer's Market.

- Practice calling the child's name and having her or him answer, "I am here."

- Practice calling, "Come here, _____" and have the child come to you immediately to get a small reward.

- Play games like "Red Light/Green Light" using the words, "Stop. Walk. Run" instead, getting rewards for following the commands.

When we go out in the world, especially as children become more independent, keeping track of them can be challenging.

Kids are safest if we know where they are, who is with them, and what they are doing. Learning to follow the Kidpower safety rule of "Check First Before You Change Your Plan" can help to prevent wandering or other unsafe behavior but often leads to disappointment. Be sure to reward your child each time she or he Checks First with you by saying enthusiastically, "GOOD JOB! THANK YOU FOR CHECKING FIRST!"

To teach how to "Check First", you can:

- Teach the Kidpower Safety Sign for "Check First" or create your own sign and practice it using with role-plays of common temptations, such as seeing a puppy or a favorite game.

- Give lots of relevant examples using pictures or actual situations or stories of when to Check First – someone you don't know calls your name, you see a funny puppet,

- Make signs by the door with reminders and drawings: "STOP! Did you ask to go outside?"

Figuring out how to balance your child's independence with safety often requires step-by-step solutions that depend on your child's abilities, age, and skills.

"Too Small
And Too Precious"

Earliest Teachable Moment

Kidpower's Underlying Principle is that: *The safety and self-esteem of a child are more important than anyone's embarrassment, inconvenience, or offense.* Basically, this means that we are committed to putting safety first, ahead of uncomfortable feelings.

A few years ago this principle was very helpful to me personally when I saw an unprotected small child in an unsafe place. A few years ago, my husband Ed and I took a vacation in Sequoia and King's Canyon National Parks in California, an area full of beautiful mountains and a great deal of wildlife.

One afternoon, I left Ed sitting by a trail and went back to the parking lot to get something for our hike. Suddenly, I noticed a small child of less than two years old sitting alone on a picnic table, next to a sign warning about this being an active bear area and no adults with her.

With her plump cheeks, sweet smile, and cute pink dress with embroidered flowers, she looked like a deeply cherished child. I could hear voices of people and splashing in the direction of the river where she was looking intently, but no one was in sight.

No part of me could have left this toddler alone there, but, especially with my husband waiting for me, I felt indignant.

I wished that parks and parking lots would have those signs that many stores do: "Do not leave your children unattended!" Surely, I thought crossly, this reminder is as important as the signs warning not to leave your valuables in your car and not to feed the bears.

I waited near this little girl for quite a while; not wanting to alarm her by staring at her or approaching her, hoping that her adults would appear. Understandably, she eventually started to get restless, so I called out towards the river, "HELLO! EXCUSE ME!"

A woman's head peeked out over the edge of the hill and called, "Is she all right?"

"She's fine," I reassured the woman. The woman's head then disappeared, as she headed back to the river. "WAIT!" I yelled. "Please come here!"

The child's mother reluctantly walked up the hill to us. She looked hot and tired and said apologetically, "I was only going to be gone for a second."

"Your child is too young and too important to be left here even for a second!" I said in a firm, kind voice.

"Really?" the woman asked.

"There are Bears," I pointed out. "And the River. And Cars. And People! You should not leave her in a place like this even for a second."

The woman lifted her child and put her on her hip. "Thank you," she said, doubtfully, and carried her daughter off to join the rest of their family.

Later, Ed and I told our story to a ranger who, with a great deal of emotion, described how children drown every year in that river because people are misled by the serenity of the surroundings into believing that it is safe.

A plan to Put Safety First makes decisions in a situation like this so clear – waiting with a child even if your husband must be wondering why you are taking so long; speaking up even if someone might be upset with you; and being supportive to a tired mother even though you feel frustrated about her lack of awareness.

The safety of kids is everybody's business, and young children are too small and too precious for us to leave them anywhere without adult protection. The article in the Appendix, *Resisting the Illusion of Safety,* describes how very caring adults can be fooled into leaving a small child unprotected for "just a minute"- near a road, outside a store, near a stove, in a car, with an animal or other young child, or near water – sometimes with harmful consequences.

Yes, we are busy, but the Put Safety First principle helps us to remember that protecting our children comes ahead of our convenience, their wishes, and anyone's offense.

Good Manners For Adults When Socializing With Young Children

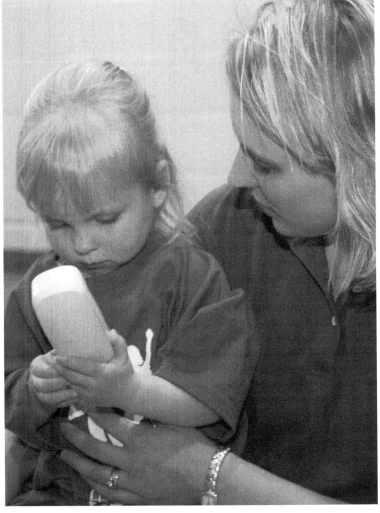

Earliest Teachable Moment

Adults are often very concerned about children using good manners. Let's turn the tables and look at what good manners are likely to mean from a younger child's point of view.

These suggestions are based on definitions of respect incorporated in Kidpower's methodology for teaching young people skills for keeping themselves and others emotionally and physically safe.

We understand that both cultures and individuals sometimes have different definitions and practices about good manners than the examples used here. What one sees as criticizing, another might see as providing crucial knowledge. What one sees as unkind joking, another might see as trying to put at ease. One might have a top priority of respecting the wisdom of elders; another's top priority might be to ensure that children are treated with respect.

According to cultural communications expert Lillian Roybal Rose, "Cultures are benign and do not inherently promote oppression of anyone. It is possible, within the context of any culture, to treat each individual with dignity and care. Practices that diminish children come from Adultism – the social oppression of children as a group - rather than from cultural differences."

In our experience, children are likely to learn more from seeing respectful behavior modeled towards themselves and their parents than from being scolded to show good manners. Good manners from adults means accepting that caring parents might make different choices, respecting boundaries that are set by parents as much as possible, having realistic expectations about children's behavior, and making affection a true choice.

Below are eight suggestions that can help build harmony and reduce stress in social settings with young children.

Respect the child's parents

Respect the child's parents by believing that they want the best for their children. Unless the parents' actions towards the child are dangerous on an immediate objective level, accept that doing something differently than you would does not make it wrong.

It is normal for family and friends to have very different strongly-held points of view about what is best for children. People often disagree about issues such as behavior expectations, health practices, food, education, religion, allowing a child to quit an instrument or sport, forcing a child to continue with an instrument or sport, allowing a child to express disagreement with an elder, spanking, and not spanking.

Most parenting decisions are a question of trade-offs rather than absolutely right or absolutely wrong. The reality is that theories of child rearing change over the years and we are learning more all the time about child development.

Find only nice things to say

Being a parent is one of our world's hardest and most important jobs. As much as possible, take the position that the child's parents are doing this job to the very best of their ability.

Try to avoid the temptation to criticize, give well-meaning advice, or make jokes about parents being too worried or over-protective. Avoid fearful messages that might come out of your own anxiety about what might go wrong. Instead, focus on the love and care that parents are giving their child and on the child's growing awareness, ability, and understanding.

One very useful technique that we practice with people of any age in Kidpower is Mouth Closed Power. Squeeze your lips together and don't say anything until you have thought about whether or not saying something is going to make things better. Ask yourself, "What positive purpose will be served by my telling this upsetting story or making this negative comment?"

Don't label children negatively

It is a sign of healthy curiosity when babies and toddlers try to put almost anything into their mouths; touch objects that are hot, sharp or fragile; climb onto things that are unstable or too high; or wander off. A young child who keeps trying to do things despite repeated adult disapproval is NOT bad, naughty, or misbehaving - just exploring how the world works. If you need to intervene, be sympathetic to the child's point of view and, if possible, offer an alternative. Limiting labels like "shy" or "careless" or "reckless" don't serve the best interest of the child - nor does a label like "good" when a child is quiet.

Let the child come to you

Babies, toddlers, and pre-schoolers can be wonderfully cute, and it's delightful when they respond to our overtures. However, many children are reserved and experience intense adult attention as highly intrusive. When you are open in a way that is engaging and fun, children will come to you when they are ready. To connect with a child, do something interesting near that child without expecting a response. Try to meet the child where he or she is by sitting down on the floor, playing with a toy, reading a picture book aloud in a vivid way, or just quietly watching the child play with gentle interest.

Forced affection is NOT love

Especially if you are related to a child, of course you love the child and want to be affectionate. It is important to remember that people can show affection in different ways. However, forced attention or affection is not an expression of love, but of emotional coercion, which is not healthy for anyone.

Remember that even a day is a long time in the life of a baby or toddler and that many children really only feel comfortable being held by their parents unless they know someone very well. Don't assume that any child will want to be kissed, hugged, or cuddled. Pay attention to the child's body language.

If a child pulls away, be glad that this child is developing a sense of boundaries instead of being offended that the child doesn't want to be held, roughhouse, or sit on your lap. You can invite affection as long as it's okay with the child's parents, and you do this in a relaxed way with no pressure.

Don't do something to a child that you would dislike having done to you

It would be considered very rude if you were to greet most adults with a pinch, grab, knuckle rub, or poke to any part of that adult's body. It would also be rude if people talked about you as if you weren't there. When in doubt, assume that something you wouldn't like done to you is something that children wouldn't like done to them.

Encourage parents to give you feedback about what does and does not work

Follow parents' guidance about what to offer the child to eat, what kinds of games might be fun to play, what language to use in talking to or around the child, etc. etc. etc. The more that a child's parents can trust that you will respect their wishes, the more positive they will feel about your relationship with their child.

Have realistic expectations

It is normal for small children to want immediate adult attention to their needs. Sure, you might wish that the child would be more interested in you or not keep interrupting the conversation, but these expectations are often unrealistic.

It is especially important to be realistic about expectations during times of transition, such as holidays. When kids are travelling and faced with overwhelming, unusual family situations, they may not be at their best, so grandparents and other family members should be kind in their assessments of what these kids' behavior is normally like.

Safety is more important than good manners

Social settings can be times when adults are distracted, and kids get hurt. Pay attention to where children are and what they are doing. Remove hazards or re-direct behavior when you can. If any child is about to do something dangerous or get hurt, stop the child immediately in a kind firm way and then calmly let the parents know what happened. Even if the child gets upset or the parents are embarrassed or offended, safety comes first.

Conclusion: Key Actions For Protecting Young Children From Harm

Earliest Teachable Moment

Young children are so vulnerable, and at times the job of keeping them safe can feel overwhelming. Here are some reminders about simple actions each of us can take to protect the babies, toddlers, and preschoolers in our lives from harm while starting to prepare them to learn how to take charge of their own safety and well-being.

Pay attention to your intuition. If you are even a little bit uncomfortable about a person or a situation involving your child, don't talk yourself out of doing whatever it takes to make sure that your child is safe. Instead of using the wishing technique and hoping that the problem will go away by itself, take action. No matter what your relationship is with someone, your job is to speak up, stick around, intervene, and keep watching until your concerns are addressed.

Be prepared for change. Once children start to move around, life with them often becomes far more complicated. Even when you are with your child all the time, you can still be surprised by how far your baby's reach is or how quickly your toddler can climb or crawl. The baby that couldn't reach that hot teacup in your hands as you sit on a couch today might well be able to do so tomorrow. A toddler who is sitting calmly on the floor one minute might try climbing out the open window the next. The child who clung to your hand yesterday might run wildly across the parking lot the next time you go out.

Stay aware and in charge. Remember that nothing substitutes for constant supervision. Young children do not have the understanding or the skills to stay away from danger, whether this is an animal, a cliff, a piece of glass, an electric outlet, a car, a flight of stairs, or a person who might be unsafe.

Too often, accidents happen right under the noses of adult caregivers. Don't get so distracted by adult conversation or using technology that you forget to watch what your children are doing - and don't give in to pressure from other parents or from grandparents to do things the way that they did.

Babies and toddlers require a great deal of attention in order to stay out of trouble. For example, they commonly want to explore the world by stuffing as much of it as they can into their mouths or other parts of their bodies. They'll try to find out what something feels or tastes like even if it's an electrical cord or the bleach bottle on our friend's laundry room floor. They'll dash to the other side of the street even if a car is coming.

"We just stopped at a garage sale," said one shaken father. "I turned my back for only a second, and he ran down the driveway. His sister, who's not much older, grabbed him just before he went into the street, just as a bunch of cars raced by. It's scary! What if she hadn't been right there? Next time, I'll hold on to him every minute."

Children need to try things out in order to learn, and they need adult support to help them do this safely.

Develop common-sense safety habits. Most accidents that happen to children are preventable. Make sure children use car seats every single time you drive, even if they don't want to. Don't look back to talk to them, text, or talk on your mobile phone while you are driving. Take toddlers out of the bathtub every time you go to answer the door or the phone, even if you plan to be gone "just a minute." Lock up poisons and sharp knives.

And never leave young children alone in a public place. Once, I was just putting my groceries in the car, when I saw a little boy asleep in the car next to mine in the parking lot.

Except for me, there were no other people around. I really had to leave, but the child was too young to be left alone. Anyone might have come along. So I waited by the car, watching the little boy, until his mother came ten minutes later. She apologized, saying the line in the store was longer than she expected. I wanted to shout at her and ask, "Don't you read the newspaper?"

Child-proof but don't depend on it always working. At age three, my daughter took a fork from the kitchen and used it to pry the safety cover off of the electric outlet in her bedroom. Wondering about her unusual silence, I walked in just as she was using the metal fork to stick her metal necklace into the outlet.

Remember that one needs to "child proof" grandparents and other adults left in charge of kids, as well as the spaces they are in.

Remember accidents can happen in an instant. When adults are in charge, their job is to stay close enough to the baby to stop any unsafe behavior the whole time and to follow your rules about where the baby is and what the baby is doing.

Watch out for doors, windows, pockets, and purses. Make sure that adults are prepared to protect the baby by closing doors and windows - and watch out for the small or sharp items or pills that might be someone's pockets or purse.

Stay calm if your child gets hurt. Accidents happen no matter how good a job we do. If your child does get hurt, take a breath and assess the situation. If your child is okay, give him some support (a hug, kiss, encouraging words, etc.) and then help him to calm down.

We want children to explore and to try things again, in a safe way, even if they may have fallen down or hurt themselves in the process. Most things children learn to do involve a few bumps, bruises or sometimes worse. We need to balance letting them have the opportunity to grow while also doing our best to keep things as safe as possible.

If your child does get badly hurt, do your best to stay very, very calm. Children respond to our anxiety and worry. We want to be clear with our body language and words that we are taking care of them and doing whatever we can to help them to get better.

Remember that young children can do more than you think. One three-year-old boy took his father's keys off the wall, climbed into the car, started the engine, put the car into drive, and rolled down the driveway, while his father was busy giving his baby sister a bath. Fortunately, the car was stopped by a small hill. This boy was just copying what he had seen his parents do many times.

Stay in charge of the people caring for your children. Remember that children, especially when they are younger, might not be able to tell you if there is a problem. Whenever or wherever we leave our children, we must make sure we feel good about the situation. Without jumping to conclusions, we should ask questions if our child acts afraid of someone. At the same time, we want to be sure that the people who care for our children are loving. If they are afraid to touch or hug our children, that would also be harmful.

Give children choices that you are comfortable with when you can. Being able to choose between the red cup or the blue cup, walking or being carried, etc., helps children develop decision-making skills and gives them a sense of power.

Make sure that the choices are close-ended and that both choices work well for you. For example, it's risky to ask,

"What do you want for breakfast?" A toddler might get her or his heart set on waffles when you don't have time to make them. You are less likely to create problems if you ask, "Do you want eggs or oatmeal for breakfast?"

Help children develop the vocabulary to say what they do and do not want. Remember that it can be frustrating to have others not understand you. Take the time to make sure that you do not jump to conclusions about what a child is trying to communicate.

For example, one little boy got so frustrated that he would cry because his mother kept confusing the word he used for "more" with the word for "potty." After she taught him some simple hand gestures to use along with each spoken word, they were able to understand each other much more easily.

Accept the right of children to be upset or have unhappy feelings even if they do not have the right to choose. Say calmly, "I understand that you are upset, but leaving the park (or being in your car seat, or changing your diaper, etc.) is not your choice."

Play in ways that build safety skills. When tickling or roughhousing, teach children that their "No!" means "No!" and their "Stop!" means "Stop!" Supervise to en-sure that people stop when they hear these words, even if the child changes her or his mind a second later.

For example, many adults like to play a monster game by pretending to be a monster and saying, "I'm going to get you!" The child says "No, you're not!" and giggles and runs away. Usually, that game ends with the adult catching the child yelling, "I got you!"

Instead, reinvent the ending of this game to help build safety skills. Try teaching the child to turn around and yell,

"STOP!" or "NO!" with their hands up in front of them with the palms facing out. Now have the monster run away whimpering. Coach the child to run to a safe person and yell, "I NEED HELP!" and have the safe person tell the child, "I will help you."

Don't allow forced affection. The Kidpower safety rule is that affection, teasing, and play should be the choice of each person, safe, allowed by the adult in charge (that's YOU), and not a secret.

Make sure that you and your child are comfortable with the way someone is playing or showing affection. Kisses, hugs, cheek-pinching, cuddling, and tickling games should be okay both with you and with your child.

Remember that younger children might need time to get used to other person unless they see them often. Respect and protect their right to choose whether or not they want to hug or kiss, even with their family. Teach children how to move away from unwanted touch or teasing and say firmly and politely, "Please stop. I don't like it." Tell the adults or other children to respect the child's wishes by listening and stopping.

Being able to set boundaries can help to improve the quality of a child's relationships. For example, a four-year-old boy, who we'll call André, learned Kidpower through our Montreal Center's day care project. A few weeks later, André was with his mother at a large family party. Lots of people were gathered together visiting, eating, and playing. Suddenly, André's mother heard her son shout, "STOP DOING THAT! I DON'T LIKE IT!"

Everyone stopped talking and turned to look. André's mother was embarrassed at first because her son was making a scene. It turned out that André's uncle had been tickling him. André kept telling his uncle to stop, but his uncle didn't listen. So André did what he'd learned and yelled loudly to get his uncle's attention.

André's mother ended up feeling really proud of her son for having the courage to speak up. André and his uncle are better friends than ever because now they know how to play in a way that works well for both of them.

Teach children not to keep secrets. Problems, any kind of touch, presents, touch, gifts, favors, treats, and other activities should not be a secret. Encourage kids to tell you about their worries. Listen to their fears compassionately, even if they seem silly.

Younger children will have a hard time understanding the difference between a surprise and a secret. It is safer to not ask them to keep anything a secret until they can really understand the difference between a safe surprise that everybody else knows about such as a gift or party and a potentially unsafe secret.

Since secrecy is a major reason why child abuse is not stopped, one of the most important things we can do to protect our children is let them know that we are here to listen. When they try to tell us something, we can stop what we're doing and pay attention. By having that kind of relationship with us now, they'll be far more likely to come to us later if someone tries to harm them.

Teach children to protect their feelings. Show them how to throw hurting words into a trash can instead of taking them into their hearts. You can help them to practice catching words that hurt and throwing the words away while saying something nice to themselves out loud. You can also teach children how to take compliments into their hearts and say, "Thank you!"

At a birthday party, one two-year-old boy was being teased about having his leg in a cast. He threw the words into his Kidpower Trash Can and said, "STOP! I am not letting your hurting words go into my body!"

Set a good example. Remember that children learn more from what they see you do than from what you tell them to do. Model being kind, using your words, controlling your temper, waiting your turn, and being careful.

Remind friends and family members to model treating themselves with respect as well. For example, suppose that your exuberant daughter loves to climb all over her older cousin who has come to visit. While normally he likes to play wild games, today he doesn't feel like it. Encourage your nephew to sound and look like he means it while telling his little cousin, "Please stop."

If your daughter doesn't listen, encourage your nephew to insist, while gently but firmly moving her away physically. He can redirect his cousin by offering an alternative that works for him. For example, "I said stop. Remember, we belong to ourselves and both of us get to choose whether to play or not. Right now, I want to sit quietly and talk. Later, we can play with your trains."

Keep a positive perspective. We have to keep a balance between being careful and not becoming so upset by fears for our children's safety that we forget to enjoy the good and beauty around us.

Almost any parent will have strong feelings about these fears. When my family was young, I went through a time of real grief when my little girl started walking. I kept remembering how I used to run all over the neighborhood visiting my friends and mourned that she would not have that kind of freedom in her childhood. I felt so badly that I couldn't give my wonderful daughter a better world to live in.

When I watched the news, I sometimes wondered if bringing children into the world was the right thing to do. There was so much horror - people starving, the threat of terrorism, awful diseases, global warming.

Finally, I told myself that if parents throughout the ages had let the problems of the world stop them from having children, none of us would have been born. I looked at my own kids, so busy, so interested, so full of life, and I knew that of course, having them was right.

I wish Kidpower had existed when my own children were small! Many, many parents and caregivers have told us that Kidpower has helped them to feel less anxiety, more confidence, and greater joy with the young children in their lives.

Instead of worrying, we can take charge to protect our children from harm. Instead of using fear to teach them about danger, we can make it fun to learn to stay safe!

Have fun and stay safe!

Earliest Teachable Moment

Appendix

kidp⊛wer®

Safety Signs for Everyone, Everywhere

Family members, caregivers, educators, and other concerned adults will often use highly varying words and ideas to explain about safety, which can be con-fusing, especially for young children or people with developmental disabilities. For this reason, we created the **Kidpower Safety Signs** to show essential personal safety skills and concepts using very simple drawings, gestures, and words. These signs help adults to be clear, accurate, and consistent so that children's comprehension and skills can develop more effectively.

Regardless of their age or abilities, the Kidpower Safety Signs have proven useful to many people including people with developmental disabilities, young children, college students, and corporate managers. They create a common language that makes it easy and fun for every-one, everywhere, to understand and communicate about staying safe with people.

Three of our twenty five Kidpower Safety Signs are on the following pages – Stay Together, Check First, and Wait! These are especially important for young children. Teach children the Safety Signs before you need to use them – and create practices that are relevant to their lives. Making a plan with the Safety Signs before doing an activity can help to prevent problems.

For example, you might put some toy kittens in a corner of the room and say cheerfully, "Let's pretend we are at the Farmer's Market, and there is someone with a box of

Earliest Teachable Moment

kittens. First, you Stay Together. This means sticking to me like glue." Make the Stay Together sign and coach the child to make the same gesture.

Practice running around the room changing directions as if you are in a store and have the child follow you, sticking next to you like glue. If a child forgets, stay cheerful rather than getting anxious and calmly coach the child to repeat the gesture and practice.

Now say, "Since you want to see the kittens, you can Check First." Make the Check First sign. Coach the child to make the same gesture and then to point to the pretend kittens and, if more verbal, to say, "Please may we see the kittens?"

Respond by saying, "Thank you for Checking First! But you have to Wait until I am done buying these apples." Make the Wait Safety Sign and coach child to repeat. Conclude by saying, "Thank you for waiting!" and take the child to pet the toy kittens.

For issues that a child struggles with, you can make a Little Book using the Safety Signs as solutions to safety concerns.

Please contact: EarliestTeachableMoment@kidpower.org for download information, directions, and copying permission for Kidpower Safety Signs and songs.

Safety Signs for Everyone, Everywhere

STAY TOGETHER

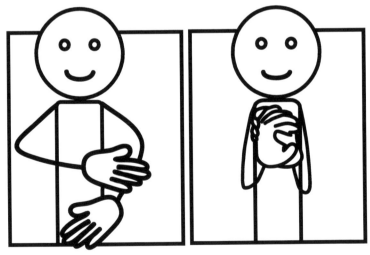

CHECK FIRST   *WAIT!*

Earliest Teachable Moment

Resist The Illusion Of Safety

Even very caring, responsible adults can be lulled into complacency by the "Illusion Of Safety." The Illusion of Safety happens in settings or situations where people feel so relaxed, sheltered, or distracted that they stop focusing on ensuring that their children have adequate supervision, understanding, and skills to avoid potential dangers. Sadly, the Illusion of Safety can lead to children being traumatized, injured, or even killed by problems that could have been prevented.

At the same time, children are likely to be less safe if their adults are constantly anxious. As adults, our challenge is to find a good balance between accepting that life is not risk free, deciding that we want children to enjoy life despite the risks, making a realistic assessment of what these risks are, and having a plan for how to avoid most of them.

Here is how to replace the Illusion of Safety with calm awareness and effective action.

Don't use the Wishing Technique or the Worrywart Technique to make decisions

We use the Wishing Technique when we trust that our wishes will make things happen or not happen the way we want. Don't give in to thoughts and statements like, "I'll just be gone for just a minute." Or, "This is a safe place. Of course, things like that don't happen here." Remember that children can come to harm within a few seconds and that "here" might mean many square miles filled with thousands of people, if it happens to be a place or a community that the adult feels attached to, such as a special annual festival. A place is only as safe as the people (or creatures) in that space are acting at any given time.

We use the Worrywart Technique when we invest time, thought, and energy worrying about all the bad things that might happen without taking any action to build skills to address our worries. The Worrywart Technique can make everyone miserable and not make children safer.

When you notice yourself or others wishing or worrying, stop and think. What is most likely to cause danger here? What kind of supervision and/or skills does my child need to be safe here?

Remember that a chain is only as strong as its weakest link

Recently, I was driving up a steep, winding road behind a school bus. I stopped when its red lights flashed, and I watched as the driver got out and, with a hand-held stop sign, carefully escorted a couple of children to the side of the street. The bus drove off, and the children started walking down the middle of this busy road, completely unaware that I was in my car right behind them. The bus driver's procedures and the lack of crime in the neighborhood helped the children be safer, but the children's own lack of skills for walking safely along a street made the situation more dangerous.

Instead of making assumptions, such as assuming that a bus driver and a peaceful neighborhood will be enough to ensure children are safe, think about all the places where a child might be and take a new look at your safety plan for each situation. Are there additional steps you can take or skills you can teach to make the situation safer?

Know who is in charge at all times

The Illusion of Safety can cause adults to trust that youth group leaders, other parents on field trips, and life guards at pools will be able to keep track of all the children they are supposed to be watching, even in crowded, chaotic places.

Adults need to be extremely direct about handing off supervision so that everyone is clear about who is in charge of each child's safety at each moment. Even children with fairly good swimming skills have drowned in hot tubs or swimming pools in the middle of a group of people because no one knew which adult was making sure that they were above water.

Also, if we are delegating the safety of our child to someone else, it is our responsibility to make sure that this person has the experience, character, skills, and enough support to do an excellent job.

Keep young children within arm's reach unless you are sure that this place is safe for them

The younger that children are, the more they are likely to lack experience, size, strength, and skill compared to most adults. They need their adults very close by to teach them how to act in the world – and to protect them from harm until they are able to protect themselves.

Even a few inches can mean the difference between having fun and having a tragedy. One very sad story happened when a four-year-old girl was hit by a car because she was just out of her mother's reach and started running to her father, who had waved to his family from the other side of the road.

For a toddler or preschooler, safety means keeping that child within arm's reach in most public places or places where there are attractive nuisances, such as animals, fountains, fans, open windows or doors, fires, friendly people, or machines. Within arm's reach means close enough to grab that child if she or he were to start moving quickly towards potential danger, such as a hot stove. Exceptions should be made on careful step-by-step basis depending on the level of risk and the capability of the child.

Watch out for distractions

At Kidpower, we ensure that our instructors focus on keeping everyone safe not just during the workshop but also that they give special attention to safety during the breaks, when adults are likely to be talking to each other and not paying attention to what their children are doing. This is why our instructors take responsibility for supervising our students at all times, even when their parents are present.

Be prepared to stop in the middle of what you are doing, abruptly interrupt a conversation, or look away from someone you are talking with in order to keep track of your child. Insist that anyone caring for your child makes staying aware of the child a higher priority than any other activity.

Prepare children for growth and change

As a child becomes more experienced, reliable, and capable, this child can start to take more responsibility for her or his own safety. The distance that it is okay to be away from the adult in charge can and should get further.

At the same time, it is important for adults to stay aware of potential hazards in new places or with new people and to provide both adequate supervision and the opportunity to practice appropriate skills for developing independence.

Remember to put Safety First

Kidpower's Underlying Principle is that "The safety and well-being of a child are more important than anyone's embarrassment, inconvenience, or offense." At times, resisting the Illusion of Safety is likely to be embarrassing, inconvenient, and annoying or offensive to ourselves, our children, and others. As adults, our job is to be realistic and to stay in charge of the safety and well-being of the young people in our lives until they are able to do this for themselves.

What Adults Need To Know About "People Safety" For Children

People Safety means being emotionally and physically safe with and around people

Strong People Safety skills help to protect children if someone acts thoughtless, mean, scary, or dangerous – and to set healthy boundaries so they can develop positive relationships that enrich their lives.

People Safety also means taking charge of their words and actions so that they act safely and respectfully towards others.

Violence against young people is a leading health issue of our time

A study about violence against children entitled "Children's Violence: A Comprehensive National Study" was released by the U.S. Department of Justice in 2009. According to the study director and director of the University of New Hampshire Crimes Against Children Research Center, David Finkelhor, Ph.D., "Children experience far more violence, abuse and crime than do adults. If life were this dangerous for ordinary grown-ups, we'd never tolerate it." The study found that over 60 percent of the children surveyed were exposed either directly or indirectly to some form of violence in the last year.

Most of the people who harm children are NOT strangers

According to the National Victims Center, 95 percent of sexual abuse happens with people children know. Of these, one third are family members – stepparents, uncles, aunts, cousins, siblings, grandparents and parents. Two thirds are other people known to the child – neighbors, youth group leaders, teachers, other children, religious leaders and friends. Experts estimate that one in three girls and one in four boys will be sexually abused before they are eighteen years old.

Molesters will often spend up to a year cultivating a trusting relationship with a family, a school, a religious community, or a group of friends before they make their first move

They will often start by systematically creating an emotional connection with a child, pushing the child's boundaries and ensuring that the child won't tell before they do anything that is sexual. This means that children who have skills for setting boundaries and getting help are less likely to be targeted by a molester.

Federal agencies estimate that there are 100,000 attempted abductions by strangers each year in the United States. About 2,000 children a year are kidnapped by strangers

Although this is important for adults to know, it is not healthy for children to believe that the world is full of dangerous people called "strangers." Instead adults can tell children that most people are good but, if we do not know them well, there are safety rules to follow.

One out of seven school children have either been victimized by bullying or have bullied others.

Most children have witnessed bullying. Bullying is harmful. Adults are responsible for noticing all forms of bullying and for taking action to make it against the rules.

Just telling children about the bad things that might happen makes them anxious

Coaching children so they can be successful in actually practicing skills helps them to become more confident and capable.

Young children are very literal, and we need to be sure that they understand what we mean

Telling children, "Never talk to a stranger" is untrue because we ask them to greet people they see as strangers all the time. Telling children, "Never let anyone touch your private areas" is also untrue because it is normal for adults to pat children, pick them up, and help them stay clean and healthy. This is why Kidpower focuses on using language that is clear, truthful, consistent, and positive.

Adults need to provide ongoing supervision to ensure the safety of the children in their lives and to keep LISTENING to children

However, it is also important that children learn how to protect themselves by knowing their safety rules and following their safety plans. Most kidnappings can be prevented if children are able to be aware, move away from someone they don't know, and check first with their adult. Most sexual abuse and most bullying can be prevented if children can set personal boundaries and ask for help. Most assaults can be stopped if children yell and run to safety when they are scared.

Kidpower helps families, schools, and youth organizations worldwide to protect their children from harm and empower young people to use their own power to stay safe.

Helicopters Or Protectors? How To Keep Your Kids Safe Without Unhelpful Hovering

When my kids were young, we worried about being "paranoid, neurotic, overprotective" parents. The popular term now is "helicopter parents" who hover over every aspect of their children's lives. Though the words are different, the phenomena are the same. As parents, we want so much for our children to be happy and safe that we have to be careful not to deprive them of opportunities to make their own mistakes, to face the consequences of unwise behavior, to learn how to overcome failure, and to develop the independence they need to become successful adults.

The problem is that fear of negative labels can get in the way of common sense. As parents or other caregivers, we don't want avoidance of being overly protective to cause us to provide too little protection. Instead of worrying about labels, we can:

- Gather information about each specific situation so that we are realistic about potential hazards.

- Trust our own intuition and judgment about when children are ready to do what.

- Help kids develop the skills and confidence they need to stay safe while becoming more independent.

- Encourage children to do things on their own as soon as they are truly ready.

Here are five questions to consider in deciding what level of involvement is enough and what is too much when you worry about whether to hover or to let go.

Is your decision based on your intuition and knowledge about what is best for your child?

Separating your intuition and good judgment from anxieties growing out of your own needs can be difficult. Parents and other caregivers sometimes have their identity become so intertwined with their children that they make decisions based on their own drive to feel safe and important rather than on what is truly best for each child. Life is not risk-free, and children's needs are different than ours. A child who is never given the opportunity to try things out on his or her own can become fearful and dependent, or rebellious and risk-taking.

One mother was terrified to let her ten-year-old daughter go on overnight visits with anyone because a friend's father had abused her as a child. Fortunately, she realized that, instead of refusing to let her daughter have fun with friends, she needed to make a plan in order to feel safe by getting to know the parents so she could trust the super-vision being provided and by being sure that her daughter had the skills to set boundaries and to get help if need be.

Are you trying to protect your child from temporary discomfort or from lasting harm?

Emotional or physical discomfort is temporary, and learning how to cope with discomfort is an essential life skill. Emotional or physical harm is lasting and can lead to injury, trauma, or even death. Our toddler can't learn to walk if we prevent him from ever falling down and being scared and hurt for a few minutes, but he needs our protection to avoid falling onto a sharp rock, out a window, or off a cliff.

Occasionally feeling sad, tired, bored, frustrated, scared, hurt, angry, or upset are all normal emotions. Children can learn that although these feelings are unpleasant, they don't need to be pushed around by them and behave in unhelpful ways. Over time, children can develop the qualities of self-control, resilience, persistence, and determination. However, being overwhelmed with these feelings much the time and struggling alone can lead to depression or other emotional damage.

Cheerfully helping children deal with discomfort is necessary in order for them to develop new skills. A child whose parents cannot tolerate her ever getting a little water up her nose while she is learning to swim may, as a result, never learn to swim. This means that she is likely to miss a lot of fun and is at greater risk of drowning.

The opposite extreme also creates problems. Suppose this child learns to swim by being thrown into the deep end of the pool where she struggles and chokes. Suppose that she is laughed at or pressured instead of being taught in a way that is safe and builds confidence. Many children taught like this become adults with a life-long fear of being in deep water. Others might love to swim but be fearful of learning other new things.

With the right kind of support, learning to walk or swim is likely to be fun even if there are moments of discomfort. The same is true with learning other skills.

Are you giving your child ongoing opportunities to learn to be more self-sufficient or constantly taking over things that your child could do?

Babies depend on their adults for everything. As children get older, adjusting to their constantly changing needs and abilities is a tricky balancing act. If we always rush to help children instead of encouraging them to do what they can for themselves as soon as they are able, we are teaching helplessness instead of building competence.

For example, children need protection from people who cross their boundaries in emotionally or physically dangerous ways. They also need opportunities to deal with uncomfortable personal situations successfully, or they will not develop their understanding of how to have successful relationships or the ability to set boundaries for themselves.

As ten-year-old Julie's mother said, "I was bullied as a child, and I could not bear the thought of anything like that happening to Julie. I was so worried that I stepped in strongly as soon as another child said a harsh word to her or even bumped into her accidentally. Julie started having trouble making friends. Finally, I realized that the problem was that she would come running to me whining as soon as she felt unhappy about anything instead of learning to work things out by speaking up for herself."

Too often adults take an "all or nothing" approach to conflict between children by either by taking over too soon and too often or by expecting kids to solve problems themselves without adequate preparation. Instead, we can give children coaching and support as they learn how to deal with conflict and build healthy relationships.

Does your child have adequate supervision and support to address potential problems?

Children need a level of supervision that is realistically based on their age, abilities, judgment, and the environment around them. They need opportunities to practice doing things for themselves within boundaries that protect them from harm as much as practically possible.

In one childcare center, three-year-old Mario was giving juicy kisses to all the children. The teachers watched Mario closely to intervene when he did this and worked with him to change this behavior. They also taught the Kidpower program to give the children practice in setting boundaries. One little girl did just what she'd learned. She noticed Mario coming, put her hands up as he approached her and yelled, "STOP!" Mario was so surprised that he completely stopped giving juicy kisses at school.

By monitoring and redirecting Mario's behavior, coaching him to listen, and preparing other kids to set boundaries, Mario's teachers turned his intrusive behavior into an opportunity for everyone to grow.

Are you assessing risks realistically rather than either denying or exaggerating them?

Gather information and then trust your own intuition and judgment. In one workshop, a mother said, "My brother let our son ride his bike alone down to the creek because he used to do this at the same age. I got horribly upset and said that our son needed to have an adult go with him. My brother told me that I am being totally paranoid. But I am overprotective, and I can't help it. Should I let my son go even though I feel so worried?"

All of the mothers and fathers there nodded their heads and said that they were also neurotic, paranoid, and overprotective. Then they all looked at me anxiously, wanting the right answer on how to fix their unreasonable feelings.

"How old is your son?" I asked the mother who had posed the question.

"Eight." she sighed.

Earliest Teachable Moment

"That's not very old," I said and then asked, "What is it like down at the creek? Is it far? Can he be safe with cars on the way there? Is it isolated? What kinds of people go down there? Has the area changed since your brother was a little boy?"

This mother's answers gave everyone a clear way to see that the creek was not a very safe place for her son without an adult with him. I then pointed out, "Our common sense tells us that we want to assess the safety of each situation carefully before making decisions about what is or is not okay for our kids. Sometimes we can become so fearful of labels like 'overprotective' or 'paranoid' or 'helicopter' that we put our common sense aside."

If you are worried about a situation, find out more. And take into consideration the knowledge, confidence, and abilities of your child as part of your assessment.

Instead of burdening ourselves with labels like "helicopter parent", we can focus on how to protect our children from harm, separate our worries from their best interests, and prepare them in positive and effective ways to develop understanding and skills.

Kidpower's Positive Practice Method gives children the opportunity to be successful in rehearsing age-appropriate skills for being safe with people in contexts that are relevant to their lives. This method also works for other important life skills.

As children tell us over and over after being confronted with a real-life problem that they have rehearsed the solution to, "I didn't have to remember because my mind and body just knew what to do!"

Practice As A Management Tool For Unsafe Or Disrespectful Behavior

When children say or do things that are hurtful, rude, destructive, or potentially dangerous, parents and teachers can find themselves trying to manage this behavior by explaining, scolding, discussing, and using rewards and punishments. Too often, these strategies make life unpleasant without solving the problem.

Practicing Kidpower skills can be a positive and effective management tool for addressing emotionally or physically unsafe behavior. Kidpower's Successful Practice Method puts the focus on what you want the children to do in order to prevent a problem like this from happening again; does not take long; does not require that you believe one party or the other; and is not punitive.

Recently, a kindergarten teacher told me how she had used the Successful Practice Method in her classroom after a little boy had kicked another in the crotch. The teacher required the boys to practice saying in a big, loud voice while making a fence with their hands, "STOP! I DON'T LIKE THIS!" She then had both boys practice using their Walk Away Power to leave. They also practiced their Hands Down Power by first imagining that they felt like touching someone or something that they shouldn't or felt like hitting, and then by using their power to pull their arms to their sides and keep them there.

This teacher reported that, later, she noticed the boy who had got kicked begin to bother the boy who had kicked him. This time, instead of kicking, he made his fence and set his boundary. The other little boy, who had meant no harm, immediately stopped!

This teacher's story inspired a skill that we now call "Feet Down Power" as a technique to help a child remember NOT to kick. To practice Feet Down Power, imagine that you really feel like kicking someone. Instead of kicking, pretend that your feet are glued to the ground and use your power to keep them there or to move them only enough that you can walk away.

Here are some Kidpower tips for how to use the Successful Practice Method as an effective, respectful behavior management tool with children:

Remember that children often want to do something that their adults think is a bad idea

Young people don't know. They forget. They experiment with testing boundaries or with negative uses of their power. Our rules are not nearly as important to children as they are to us. Instead of seeing "bad" behavior as a failure for ourselves or our children, we can use these problems as opportunities for children to learn. The point of having them practice skills is not to punish them but to give them chances to show how they can use their skills to handle real-life situations.

Set a good example by accepting and managing your upset feelings

Whether your toddler just climbed high up a ladder or your teenager swore at her mother, getting upset about emotionally destructive or physically dangerous behavior is completely normal. Rather than trying to suppress your feelings of annoyance, sadness, shock, worry, frustration, or anger when your child does something upsetting, accept your right to have these feelings. And then, in order to deal with the problem safely and effectively, manage your feelings instead of letting them cause you to shut down, get frantic, or explode.

You can practice for yourself by imagining your child doing something dangerous or destructive and then getting centered. Take a deep breath. Feel where your hands and feet are. Straighten your back. Look at or imagine seeing something calming. Remember that you can choose to look at the problem behavior as a chance for everyone to strengthen relationships and learn important life skills.

Don't lecture or argue

Suppose that two kids are fighting and you didn't see it start. Avoid playing the judge and deciding whose story to believe. Instead, you can point out that they were both doing something unsafe – fighting – and that you want to see each of them practice how to make safe choices. Then, coach them to practice skills such as: using their awareness to notice that someone is getting upset; saying, "Please stop"; stopping when someone sets a reasonable boundary; walking away; using Hands Down Power and Mouth Closed Power; and getting help.

Address resistance with creativity, compassion, and humor

How many of us really like being told that you've done something wrong? Most of us hate it, and most kids feel the same way. Resistance can include:

- Saying, "I don't want to!" and protesting bitterly.

- Rolling eyes and sighing heavily.

- Making rude remarks and sarcastic jokes.

- Arguing or minimizing with comments like, "I said I'm sorry so why are you punishing me?" Or, "I already know, and this is a big waste of time!"

Rather than taking a young person's resistance personally or getting stuck trying to talk her or him into agreeing with you, you can calmly persist with compassion, creativity, and humor. You can communicate a message along the lines of, "I understand. However, no matter how this problem started, I felt that what happened was unsafe (unkind, against our values, etc.). I appreciate what you are saying, but you are more likely to remember if we practice."

Your goal is to make practicing interesting and even fun, rather than to "punish" the child. For a younger child, you could start with a demonstration with puppets or toys to show the problem behavior and then to show safer choices. You could let older children or teens "practice" using spice jars or other unlikely objects as characters to act out the problems themselves and to show different safe and unsafe options. You might act out the practice yourself first; then, have your child take a turn.

Making it clear that you see the problem as something separate from the child that you can both work to solve can reduce any defensiveness or resistance on your child's part.

Find opportunities to turn problems into practices

People tell us they are using practice to address many kinds of unsafe behavior. For example, a parent with a toddler who was always running off told her child before going to the store, "It is not safe for you to leave my side when we go to the park or the store. Let's practice staying together. If you don't want me to hold onto you, then you need to show me how you can hold onto me." They practiced, and, with some reminding, her toddler held onto her.

Sometimes, people worry that the language we teach children to use does not sound like what "real children" would normally say. As adults, our job is to teach children how to behave in ways that often don't come naturally to them so that they can stay safe, have positive relationships, and get the most out of their lives. We encourage children to try using our language and then to find words that work for them as long as these are both clear and respectful.

Here are a few examples of practices that can help address problem behaviors:

Problem: Two preschoolers are playing doctor too intimately.

- **Practice 1:** Both children show how to doctor without taking off clothes or touching private areas.

- **Practice 2:** Each child says, "Stop! That's not safe!"

- **Practice 3:** Each child uses Hands Down Power to stop.

Problem: Two children are roughhousing in a way that was fun at first but then got overwhelming for one of them. One is crying, and the other is calling him a "crybaby".

- **Practice 1:** Each child says, "Stop that game! I don't feel comfortable. Let's play something else."

- **Practice 2:** Each child pretends to want to keep roughhousing, but uses Hands Down Power, Feet Down Power, and Mouth Closed Power.

- **Practice 3:** Each child uses the Trash Can to throw away the word "crybaby". Each child practices saying out loud, "My feelings are important."

Problem: Two children are shouting insults at each other.

- **Practice 1:** Each child practices taking the power out of hurtful words or insulting behavior by throwing insults away into a trash can and replacing them with kind words they take into their hearts.

- **Practice 2:** Adult pretends to be insulting by shaking a forefinger in a scolding way and yelling, "Blah! Blah! Blah!" Each child practices Walking Away with an aware, calm, respectful, and confident attitude.

- **Practice 3:** Children both pretend that they feel upset and then practice using Calm Down Power by taking a breath, straightening their backs, pressing their palms together or against their legs, and wiggling their toes.

Sometimes, more complex social dynamics have developed that require separating the children for different kinds of practices. Suppose one child is constantly being left out of games, conversations, and other activities by the other children. Unfortunately, this child whines a lot, wants to get her way all the time, and makes put-down remarks about other children, which is why they say it's not fun to play with her.

Practices for the child being left out: Speaking in a regular voice rather than whining. Using Mouth Closed Power instead of making put-down remarks. Waiting your turn. Asking in a cheerful voice, "Excuse me. Can I play?" Apologizing and persisting in the face of rejection by saying with a cheerful, assertive attitude, "I know I've sometimes been impatient and rude. I'm sorry. I'm working on changing. I'd really like to play!" Getting help using a regular voice and being specific about what happened without being attacking or insulting.

Practices for the other children in being inclusive while taking care of themselves: Giving people another chance even when you don't feel like it by saying 'yes' together with a boundary, such as, "Yes, but no hitting." Stopping people without attacking them when they say or do something that is rude. Saying, "That was a rude thing to say. Please stop!" Saying, "Excuse me! It's MY turn now." Saying, "Please use a regular voice." When things get stuck, getting help using a regular voice, and being specific about what happened without being attacking or insulting.

In addition to addressing behavior problems, the Successful Practice Method can be helpful for many other potential challenges: meeting new people when you go to a new place; recovering from a mistake when you are playing a sport without feeling bad about yourself or blaming someone else; asking someone to dance at a party; preparing for an important interview; etc. The steps are:

- Define the problem or challenge in objective terms, without judging others' character or intent

- Identify, very specifically and realistically, what you want to see happen

- Rehearse the behavior necessary to make the outcome you want possible, with coaching in how to do this effectively

SongPower!
A Fun Way To Reinforce Safety Rules And Skills

Most young children love to sing. Singing is a great way to express strong feelings and to remember important ideas.

Entertainer and psychologist Peter Alsop, Ph.D., has created many fun and thoughtful songs about life, safety, problems, and joy for young children as well as for people of all ages. His song *My Body's Nobody's Body But Mine* is used by child abuse prevention programs around the world. In 1994, Peter Alsop created a performance for Kidpower with his songs and our practices. His *Wake-Up* video, in which I appeared with Kidpower Co-Founder Timothy Dunphy and the late actor John Ritter, won an Indie Best Children's Award.

Our Montreal Kidpower Center created the first Kidpower song, which we then made a version of in English. Currently, our dynamic New Zealand Kidpower Center is creating a CD of children's songs for preschoolers. Our New Zealand Center Co-Director Cornelia Baumgartner created a *If you have Kidpower and you know it* song to the tune of *If you are happy and you know it* along with Safety Signs as gestures to make this a fun activity for four and five-year-olds.

Please contact: EarliestTeachableMoment@kidpower.org
for download information, directions, and copying permission
for Kidpower songs and Safety Signs

7 Kidpower Strategies For Keeping Your Child Safe

Put Safety First. Kidpower's core principle is:

The safety and healthy self-esteem of a child are more important than anyone's embarrassment, inconvenience, or offense.

Child protection requires putting safety first. Don't let inconvenience, embarrassment, or fear of offending someone stop you from staying in charge of the emotional and physical safety of your child.

Keep your radar on. Stay in charge of what is happening with your kids. Insist that all caregivers and professionals provide powerful, respectful adult leadership. Remember that people who are a danger to kids usually look and act very nice. Don't let your kids be in places where you are not welcome. Drop in unexpectedly.

Pay attention to your intuition. If you feel uncomfortable or your gut makes you worry that something might be wrong, insist on answers. Notice if someone seems to be singling your child out for special gifts or favors or time alone.

LISTEN to your children and teach them not to keep unsafe secrets. Problems, touch, gifts, favors, and activities should NOT be a secret. Ask occasionally in an interested, calm way, "Is there anything you've been wondering or worrying about that you haven't told me?"

Stay calm and caring when kids talk with you about problems so that they feel safe coming to you.

Make SURE Kids know you CARE. Don't assume that a child knows. No matter how busy you are, tell young people often, "Your safety and well being are very, VERY important to me. Even if I seem too busy, or you made a mistake, or someone we care about will be upset, or you feel embarrassed, if anything bothers you, I want to know. Please tell me and I will do everything in my power to help you."

Show you care by listening compassionately even if a concern seems silly to you. Avoid the temptation to lecture or point out mistakes. Take action by helping your child figure out options or, if this is a problem that needs adult attention, by advocating for your child in a way that sets a good example for how to resolve problems respectfully, powerfully, and persistently.

Don't let kids throw stones. Intervene immediately so that you stop a child being unkind to another with the same determination that you would stop that child from throwing a rock through a window.

Every adult in charge of children is responsible for ensuring that each child stays emotionally and physically safe and that this child acts safely and respectfully towards others. Model being firm, kind, and persistent when you intervene.

Assess your child and make Safety Plans. Assess realistically the capabilities and vulnerabilities of your child. Make a list of everywhere your child goes, what kinds of problems he might encounter, and how she would avoid the problem and get help if necessary. Before you let your child go anywhere without adult protection, make sure that your child is prepared with sufficient knowledge, skills, and life experience.

Prepare children to take charge of their safety by practicing skills. One quick action can stop most abuse and bullying – using your awareness, checking first, moving away from trouble, acting confident, pushing someone's hand away, ordering someone to stop, leaving as soon as you can, resisting emotional coercion, and being persistent in telling until you get help.

Kids are more likely to be able to take actions like these when they need to if they understand their safety rules and have the chance to rehearse using these skills in a fun, age-appropriate way.

Advocating With Family Members For Your Kids

Parents often approach Kidpower for coaching and support when they have concerns about the behavior of family members or close friends around their children. Speaking up for our kids is important – and, although we can't control how others respond, making thoughtful choices about HOW we speak up can increase the chances that the communication will be more positive and productive.

Here are a few typical stories describing how parents have advocated for their kids with family members or prepared their children to take charge of the problem themselves. A few details have been changed to protect privacy, but the stories are true.

"My grandmother smokes, and I just couldn't let her do this near our baby. Even though her feelings were hurt, I said that we would need to visit in a room that was not smelling of smoke. It was inconvenient, but I found a place nearby where we could get together, and where she could smoke in another room if she needed to."

"My father-in-law kept threatening to spank my four-year-old daughter, even though he knows we don't hit kids in our family. It was very upsetting. Finally, I gathered my courage and, with my husband standing next to me, told my father-in-law that I know he loves his grandchildren very much and means well, but that it is not okay to threaten to hit our kids or to tell us that we should be spanking them. My husband told his father that he agreed with me. At first, my father-in-law was angry, but he did change his behavior, and we are much less stressed during visits."

"We have long-time friends who are like family to us. When we get together, their six-year-old daughter is always trying to play with our three-year-old daughter alone. Our daughter, who adores this older girl, told us that her friend wanted to play doctor, tried to take off her clothes, and said she should keep it a secret. My friends say that this is just normal play for kids, but I said that we need to keep the children with us and supervise until we're confident they won't keep touch a secret or ask each other to keep touch a secret. Our friends are deeply offended."

"My sister's pre-teen daughter kept teasing my five-year old son at our family gatherings, poking fun at him until he was in tears. My sister says kids should just work things out themselves. After worrying for days, I told my sister that I wanted a "no unkind teasing" rule at family events. She told me I was over-sensitive and making my son into a 'sissy', but I insisted. Eventually, she agreed to talk with her daughter."

"At the dinner table, my brother-in-law suddenly started knuckling my ten-year-old son's head in a way that was painful. I've given my son permission to get up from the table and move to a different chair if his uncle tries to do this again. I said if anyone got upset, his father and I would back him up."

"I have two aunts who kept giving my teenagers the inquisition about what they are doing in school or how much they eat or weigh until they were unhappy about going to any family gathering. Finally, I gave my teens permission to change the subject and not answer questions or continue unpleasant conversations by saying in a polite voice, 'Excuse me. I want to talk about something else.' I told them they could then start talking about a neutral topic like a favorite movie. We practiced, and, although they had

Earliest Teachable Moment

to do it over and over, this approach worked like a charm at the next holiday dinner."

"My husband's nephew is fifteen years old. He's a sweet kid, but I feel uncomfortable about how he is treating my five-year-old daughter. He wants to cuddle with her for a long time, whisper to her almost like a girl friend, and go off with her alone. I know my sister-in-law would have a fit if I implied that anything inappropriate might be going on. I am going to make sure that I keep my daughter in sight whenever he visits and explain that she needs to Check First with me before leaving the room."

Our children's job is to get out of difficult situations as best they can and to tell us when they have problems. As adults, our job is to stay aware of what our kids are doing, to be advocates for them when they need it, to teach them skills, and to create safe environments for them. Even if we can't make a situation better right away, our children need to know that we take them seriously and that we are doing whatever we can to fix the problem.

Staying calm, firm, respectful, and persistent when speaking up to family members can be challenging especially because they know how to push all our buttons. Personally, I don't like being told what to do or that I did something wrong and have to work hard not to react poorly if someone says I am doing something wrong.

In our workshops, we use the following role-play to demonstrate how to persist in the face of common negative reactions. We set the stage by explaining that this is a discussion between one of four-year-old Monique's parents and her or his parent, who often takes care of the granddaughter Monique. The negative reactions and positive responses are in bold.

Parent: "Dad (or Mom), I want to talk with you about Monique."

Grandpa: "Wonderful! I love that kid!"

Parent: "She loves you too, and I really appreciate how much you're helping me out by taking care of her. There's just one problem."

Grandpa: "Oh, really? What is it?"

Make a bridge with I feel... When you... Would you please.
Parent: "I know that you mean well, and I feel concerned that Monique is starting to feel badly about herself when you tease her so much. Please try not to call her names."

Denial. Grandpa: "What are you talking about? I never do that!"

Giving a specific example. Parent: "It's possible you don't notice, but it happens. Just yesterday you called her "butterfingers" when she spilled her juice."

Minimizing. Grandpa: "Oh that. That's just a game. She likes it."

Acknowledge his reality, explain why his behavior is a problem, restate boundary. Parent: "I understand that it's a game to you, but she's starting to think of herself as clumsy. Please stop calling Monique names."

Emotional coercion. Grandpa: "How can you talk to me like this? You're making a big deal out of nothing, as usual."

Calmly and kindly acknowledge feelings. Parent: "You sound upset."

More guilt. Grandpa: "You bet I'm upset! Hey, I know what this is about! You feel jealous because I get to spend more time with her than you do!"

Keep acknowledging. Parent: "I realize this is upsetting for you, and I'm sorry this is hard. I appreciate your talking with me."

Violating the boundary. Grandpa: "I know what I'm doing. After all, I raised you. You turned out just fine. (At this point, half the people in the room are often gritting their teeth and thinking, "Yeah, and she's spent years in therapy recovering!") I'm her grandfather! I'll do whatever I want when I'm with her."

Acknowledge feelings, explain importance, and state a consequence. Parent: "I'm sorry this is so upsetting for you, but the way the world is nowadays, children have to know that their feelings will be respected by the people they most love. Unless you can agree to try to stop calling her names, I can't let Monique stay so much with you."

Shutting down. Grandpa: (head down, turning away) "I can't talk about this anymore."

Express caring. Parent: "I'm sorry this is so hard for you, Dad. I really hope we can work this out."

Stays shut down. Grandpa: "I don't know. I'll talk it over with your Mom."

Hopefully, after getting some perspective, Grandpa will make an effort to respect his adult child's wishes about avoiding teasing his granddaughter experiences as hurtful.

As this story shows, speaking up often doesn't work out easily right away. Most people don't like to be told that they have to change. Here are some guidelines that can help these difficult conversations go as well as possible.

- Do not use text, e-mail, or any other form of messaging. A caring and respectful tone of voice and an interactive conversation are essential in preventing unnecessary problems. Communicating boundaries in a way that does not involve face-to-face or direct voice communication is likely to make problems worse, not better.

- Prepare, so that you know exactly what you want to say and the specific changes you want to see. Write down what you want to say, what you think the negative reactions are likely to be, and how you plan to persist in a powerful and respectful way instead of getting upset.

- Arrange a quiet time and private place for the conversation by saying, "I have a concern I want you to talk about."

- Be together with your partner, if possible, if you are communicating boundaries to your partner's family member. Plan with your partner so that, ideally, your partner will be prepared to back you up.

- Acknowledge the other person's good intentions or perspective by starting with a bridge such as, "I know you want the best." Or, "I know how busy you are."

- Set the boundary in non-attacking terms. State your feelings, what the specific behavior is that concerns you, and what you want to see change.

- Don't get defensive or hooked into talking about side issues if the other person is negative. Just acknowledge any upset feelings and restate your boundary. Stay focused on what you want to see change rather than getting distracted by attacking remarks or behavior.

- Be prepared to state a consequence, if need be, if the behavior doesn't change.

- Don't insist on immediate resolution or agreement, unless it is an emergency,. Allow the other person some time to save face and think things over unless doing so will directly affect someone's safety.

- Have a plan about what you will do if the other person doesn't change his or her behavior, including restricting access or, in serious situations, even disengaging from the relationship.

- If you wish you had done something differently, apologize sincerely for this piece of what you said or did, even if the other person said or did something much worse. However, don't retract your boundaries about what needs to change.

- Congratulate yourself on having the courage to speak up. Remember our Kidpower saying that you do not have to be perfect to be GREAT!

Kidpower Services For All Ages and Abilities

Workshops

Through our active centers and travelling instructors, Kidpower has conducted workshops in over sixty countries spanning six continents. Our programs include: Parent/Caregiver Education seminars; Parent-Child workshops; Weekend Family Workshops; classroom and teacher training programs; Teenpower self-defense workshops for teens; Collegepower for young people leaving home; Fullpower self-defense and boundary-setting workshops for adults; Seniorpower for older people; adapted programs for people with special needs; training for professionals; and workplace violence prevention and communication programs.

Our three-day Child Protection Skills Institute provides professionals and parents with training in how to use our program in their personal and professional lives.

Free on-line library

Our extensive on-line Library provides over 100 free "People Safety" resources including articles, videos, webinars, blog entries, and podcasts. We regularly send new resources directly to our subscribers through our Kidpower e-newsletters. Free downloads for personal use are available of our Kidpower Safety Signs, coloring book, and articles. We provide licensing for use of materials or content for charitable or educational purposes.

Books

We provide an extensive K-12 curriculum that many families, schools, and youth organizations use in their own prevention and child protection programs to keep kids safe from bullying, abuse, kidnapping, and other violence. We also have manuals for training teens and adults. For a full list, please visit our online Bookstore.

- *The Kidpower Book for Caring Adults*, a comprehensive guide for understanding personal safety, self-protection, confidence, and advocacy for young people.

- Cartoon-illustrated *Safety Comics* series for younger children, older children, and teens or adults.

- *Preschool to Young Adult Curriculum Teaching Books.*

- *Bullying: What Adults Need to Know and Do to Keep Kids Safe.*

- *Fullpower Relationship Safety Skills Handbook for Teens and Adults.*

- *15 People Safety Group Lessons - Teaching children how to be safe with people.*

- *One Strong Move: A Cartoon-Illustrated Introduction to Teaching Self-Defense to Children, Teens, and Adults.*

- *The Kidpower Skills for Child Protection Workbook -* textbook from our three-day Institute.

Coaching, consulting, and curriculum development

Long-distance coaching by video-conferencing, telephone, and e-mail enables us to make our services accessible worldwide. We consult with organizations and schools on how to best adapt our program to meet their needs and develop new curriculum to increase the "People Safety" knowledge of different groups facing difficult life challenges.

Instructor Training and Center Development

Our very comprehensive training program prepares qualified people to teach our programs and to establish centers and offices for organizing services in their communities under our organizational umbrella.

Acknowledgements

This book is possible thanks to **Amanda Golert**, our Kidpower Sweden Center Director, Training and Curriculum Consultant, and Senior Program Leader whose talented design and production skills have taken several collections of writing and turned them into a real book.

Lessons from all of the children in my life and all their adults have taught me a great deal about treating children with respect, keeping them safe, protecting their well-being, and teaching them how to take charge of their own safety and well-being.

I want to thank everyone in our Kidpower community for your tremendous commitment and generous contributions of expertise, time, money, skills, ideas, and stories. Thanks to you, we have created a joyful, effective personal safety program that has protected and empowered people of all ages and abilities all over the world. Special thanks go to:

- **Timothy Dunphy**, our Program Co-Founder, who was crucial in bringing Kidpower into being and who still teaches with love and laughter.

- **Erika Leonard**, our California Program Director and Senior Program Leader, who helped put together our first Kindle book, *Early Childhood 101*, which is now incorporated in this book.

- **Chantal Keeney**, our Senior Program Leader and Senior Instructor, for providing important editing and examples about working with young children.

- **Cornelia Baumgartner**, New Zealand Center Co-Director, for the song *"If You Have Kidpower and You Know It"*.

- **John Luna-Sparks**, Kidpower Senior Instructor and Program Leader and Psychotherapist, for important additions for parents with kids who struggle with staying safe with their bodies.

- **Lynn Brown**, Kidpower UK Center Co-Director and Instructor and psychotherapist, for her careful editing and thoughtful suggestions.

- **Lisa Piper**, for the beautiful Kidpower bear photo on the front cover and the photo on page 128. **Claire Laughlin** for the photo on page 3. **Miki Yannoni** for the photos on page 15 and 100. John Luna-Sparks and **Jeff Luna Sparks** for the photo on page 21. **Lynn Brown** and **Colin Stewart** for the photos on page 29, 74 and 118. **Zaida Torres** for the photo on page 35. **Antonie del Bonta** for the photo on page 70 and **Natalie Younger** for the photo on page 111.

Long ago, when I wrote my first book, which was for parents and caregivers of toddlers, my eight-year-old daughter announced proudly, "Me and my little brother taught her everything she knows!" My own children definitely inspired that book and many others – and were the inspiration for starting Kidpower as well.

By the way, that first book was called, *1,2, 3… The Toddler Years* – and by now I'd probably be writing a book called *29, 30, and Beyond… The All Grown Up But Still My Kids Years* – but Kidpower happened instead.

About The Author

Irene van der Zande is the Founder and Executive Director of Kidpower Teenpower Fullpower International, a global non-profit leader dedicated to protecting people of all ages and abilities from bullying, violence, and abuse by empowering them with knowledge and skills.

Since 1989, Kidpower has served over 2.5 million children, teenagers, and adults, including those with special needs, through its positive and practical workshops, extensive free online Library, and publications.

Since Kidpower began, Irene has led the development of programs, training of instructors, and establishment of centers, working with a wide range of international experts in education, public safety, violence prevention, mental health, and the martial arts.

Irene has authored numerous books and articles in the child development, child protection, positive communication, and violence and abuse prevention and intervention fields, including:

The Parent/Toddler Group: A Model of Effective Intervention to Facilitate Normal Growth and Development, which is published by Cedars-Sinai Medical Center and used as a textbook for mental health and child education professionals; *1, 2, 3... The Toddler Years: A Guide for Parents and Caregivers*, which is used as a textbook in early childhood development programs in many colleges and has a foreword by early childhood development and Respect for Infant Educarers founder Magda Gerber; *The Kidpower Book for Caring Adults*, a comprehensive guide on personal safety, self-protection, confidence, and advocacy for young people; *Bullying – What Adults Need to Know and Do To Keep Kids Safe*, which is used in the anti-bullying programs of many families, schools, and youth organizations; and the cartoon-illustrated Kidpower *Safety Comics Series* and *Preschool to Young Adult Curriculum Teaching Books*, which provide entertaining and effective tools for introducing and practicing safety skills with young people.